WADSWORTH PHII

ON

MODERN PHILOSOPHY

Garrett Thomson
College of Wooster

Australia • Canada • Mexico • Singapore • Spain • United Kingdom • United States

Printed in Canada
1 2 3 4 5 6 7 07 06 05 04 03

Printer: Transcontinental-Louiseville

ISBN: 0-534-25245-1

For more information about our products, contact us at:
Thomson Learning Academic Resource Center
1-800-423-0563

For permission to use material from this text, contact us by:
Phone: 1-800-730-2214
Fax: 1-800-730-2215
Web: www.thomsonrights.com

For more information contact:
Wadsworth-Thomson Learning
10 Davis Drive
Belmont, CA 94002-3098
USA

Asia
Thomson Learning
5 Shenton Way #01-01
UIC Building
Singapore 068808

Australia/New Zealand
Thomson Learning
102 Dodds Street
Southbank, Victoria 3006
Australia

Canada
Nelson
1120 Birchmount Road
Toronto, Ontario M1K 5G4
Canada

Europe/Middle East/South Africa
Thomson Learning
High Holborn House
50-51 Bedford Row
London WC1R 4LR
United Kingdom

Latin America
Thomson Learning
Seneca, 53
Colonia Polanco
11560 Mexico D.F.
Mexico

Spain/Portugal
Paraninfo Thomson Learning
Calle/Magallanes, 25
28015 Madrid, Spain

CONTENTS

	Preface	v
1.	Introduction: The End of an Era	1

PHASE ONE

2.	The Rise of Science: Copernicus to Galileo	8
3.	Bacon and the New Map of Knowledge	16
4	Descartes: The Unity of Science	23
5.	Descartes and Elizabeth: The Nature of Humans	37
6.	Early Modern French Philosophy	42
7.	Hobbes: Politics as Science	49
8.	Spinoza: Against Dualism	55
9.	Newton: The Grand Vision	66
10.	Locke and the Proper Business	70
11.	Locke: A Reasonable Revolutionary	85
12.	Interim conclusion: The State of Play	91

PHASE TWO

13.	Leibniz: New Questions	97
14.	Leibniz: From Physics to Theology	106
15.	Berkeley: The Denial of Matter	112
16.	Hume: Skepticism and Naturalism	122
17.	Hume: The Slave of the Passions	130
18.	Interim Conclusion: The Need for Synthesis	136

PHASE THREE

19.	The French Enlightenment	140
20.	Kant: The Transcendental Turn	145
21.	Kant: From Theory to Practice	167
22.	Kant: Toward Romanticism	178
23.	Grand Conclusion: A Failed Project?	186
	Bibliography	194

Preface

The philosophy of the modern period, which stretches from roughly 1600-1800, is one of the most interesting and urgent for us to study. During this period, humanity's conceptions of itself and the universe altered radically mainly because of the rise of science and the implications of this for knowledge, ethics and politics. It was a time of many revolutions, transformations and innovations.

Furthermore, many of the philosophical problems of the modern period are still with us today. Much contemporary philosophical thinking is a struggle to free ourselves of some of the assumptions of the modern period. However, it is very much a contentious matter which of those assumptions we should relinquish and which we should retain. For these reasons, the study of modern philosophy is important for understanding the philosophy of the twenty-first century.

This book is intended to compliment my own earlier book *Bacon to Kant: An Introduction to Modern Philosophy*. In that book, I tried to present the arguments and conclusions of the major philosophical figures and assess their value. In this book, I shall try to present a more complete picture of modern philosophy as a historical and social process. For example, there is an extended chapter on the historical events leading to the modern period and another on the early modern scientific thinkers, such as Copernicus and Galileo. This book is organized historically rather than thematically.

In this work, I have tried to characterize the development of modern thought more holistically. For example, I have included some of the main ethical and political theories of the time. Also, there are three chapters in which I stand back from the arguments of the individual philosophers to examine the development and significance of modern philosophy as a whole.

Also in this volume, I intend to present lucidly the aims of each of the thinkers concerned and their basic strategy for achieving those aims in the context of their lives. I intend to do this for two reasons. First, this helps us to understand their thought much more easily. This will be the principle around which I shall organize their arguments so that their goals are clear. In this way, it is harder for students to become lost in details and easier for them to appreciate the relevance of the arguments. Second, this also helps to assess critically the basic assumptions of these arguments at a more fundamental level.

This approach also requires a more comprehensive biography of the philosophers. Each thinker has a style of philosophy defined by the individual's aims and strategy, and these are best understood in the context of their lives.

In contrast to my earlier work, in this volume I do not evaluate critically the conclusions of the philosophers. Nor do I indicate the weaknesses of their arguments. This is not because I think that their theories and arguments should not be criticized. It is rather because the current volume is directed exclusively to explanation. If you would like more critical evaluation, please use my other work *Bacon to Kant.* If you prefer more contextualized explanations and feel that criticism is best undertaken in the classroom, you will prefer this book.

Of course, this book does contain criticisms by the modern philosophers themselves, such as Kant's criticism of Descartes and Empiricism and Leibniz's critique of Locke. Furthermore, in this volume, I provide a critical appreciation of modern thought as a whole in order to help the reader identify some common characteristics and assumptions of the philosophy of the period. This should help students begin to relate modern philosophy to more contemporary debates.

In writing this book, I have relied on other works of my mine published by Wadsworth Press. In particular, I have borrowed sections from *On Descartes*, *On Locke*, *On Leibniz* and *On Kant*, all published previously by Wadsworth. There are, though, substantial differences. First, where I have found a way to explain an argument or thesis more clearly and lucidly, I have used it. For example, my expositions of Descartes and Leibniz are quite different. When I have not found a clearer explanation, I have used earlier material. Furthermore, as I mentioned before, in this volume I have tried to characterize the period as a whole.

1

Introduction: The End of an Era

For convenience, we can mark the beginning of the modern and the end of the medieval eras with the date 1600. However, the enormous transformations of the modern period, which saw the birth of science and the rise of the nation state, have their prelude in a series of earlier and slower changes, which we need to chronicle briefly in this first chapter by way of an introduction.

The year 1000 was a turning point in medieval Europe. There was relatively more political security and less threat from invading pagan hordes. This led to more cultural and economic activity, to more and bigger towns with an emerging middle class, and to improvements in agriculture. The ideals of knightly chivalry replaced those of the warrior of the earlier period. The Catholic Church dominated this emerging medieval civilization. Three series of events signal and symbolize the dimensions of this mastery.

First, the Church achieved political dominance. In 800, Pope Leo III crowned King Charlemagne of France as emperor of Europe. This act symbolized the idea that kings rule by the grace of God as represented by the Church. Of course, there were conflicts between the Popes and various kings and emperors, especially the rulers of the German Empire. For example, there was the famous struggle between Henry IV and Pope Gregory VII regarding the Pope's ruling that all bishops should be appointed by the Church. When Henry was excommunicated in 1077, he was forced to stand barefoot outside a castle in the snow for the three days and to beg for Papal forgiveness.

However, after regaining power, Henry retaliated, sending an army to Rome and deposing Gregory. Nevertheless, despite such power struggles, the fact remained that the Pope crowned emperors and could excommunicate them. For example, in 1213, Innocent III (1198-1216) forced King John to surrender England to papal domination.

Second, the Church achieved cultural and spiritual dominance. In 529, St. Benedict founded the first Benedictine monastery and formed the Benedictine Rule as a guide to monastic life. The Benedictines spread Christianity throughout Europe, and their order, like the Church itself, grew very wealthy. The Church owned almost one third of all land in Europe. As a consequence, the vitality of its spiritual mission became lost. The Benedictine Rule was often bent or ignored. The founding of the Dominican and Franciscan orders, both around the year 1210, imported new monastic ideals into Christianity, thereby revitalizing it. Furthermore, the Church embraced the popular veneration of the Virgin Mary as part of its own culture; it became the 'Holy Mother Church.' Mary embodied many distinctively Christian virtues, such as purity, modesty and love, which also were part of medieval chivalry. At the same time, Mary became the sympathetic, maternal and protective mediator between humanity and the sterner figure of Christ. Additionally, the new wealth and stability of Europe after 1000 led to the founding of the first universities initially dedicated to the study of theology. In the 15th century, there was a growing tide of devotional and mystical feeling in Europe, especially the Rhineland. People were seeking a direct contact with the divine and new answers to spiritual questions. Although this movement contained the seeds of the later Reformation, because of the factors mentioned above, the Church was able to maintain its spiritual leadership. In short, the Church was the spiritual and cultural center of this new medieval society.

Third, the Church achieved intellectual dominance by thwarting a threat. When the Islamic Moors invaded Spain and Italy in 700- 800, they brought into Europe some of the incredibly rich and varied culture of ancient Greece, which had been lost after the fall of the Roman Empire, around the time of St. Augustine (354–430). Slowly, the influence of these ancient texts spread north. During the 13th century, as more and more of Aristotle's writings were translated, medieval thinkers began to hold his works in awe. This is why Aristotle was called 'the master of all those who know.' The interpretations of the logical and scientific works of Aristotle by the Arabic thinkers, Avicenna and Averroes, were especially influential. As a result, new heresies began to emerge in the 13th century. In response, the Church asked various thinkers, including St. Thomas Aquinas to reply, and to defend intellectually Christian belief. Aquinas (1226–1274) invented a new dogma, which replaced the earlier Platonic philosophy of St. Augustine. In this way, the Catholic Church managed to harness Aristotle and thereby, averted a philosophical revolution and solidified its intellectual position. In effect, Aquinas made Aristotle Christian and made Christianity Aristotelian. Fifty years after his death, he was canonized, and. his teaching became the new dogma, which was vividly portrayed in Dante's *Divine Comedy*. Aquinas' *Summa Theologica* became the main textbook for instruction in theology.

To appreciate the centrality of the Catholic Church in medieval Europe, it is necessary to consider some other points. First, there was the very real fear of Hell. In 1215, the Lateran Council declared that no one could be saved outside of the Church. The fear of Hell exercised a tremendous influence on the medieval imagination and, consequently, so did the Church's story of redemption and salvation. Furthermore, most people had very hard and short lives. The Christian idea of Heaven provided much needed hope. Second, the Church dominated the landscape of Europe. There was a church in every village and, in the cities, magnificent Gothic cathedrals. In summary, at the height of its power in medieval Europe, the Roman Catholic Church had incredible success in its worldly mission, and the continuity of Western culture was due to this success.

The Beginnings of Change

However, history is never static. The later medieval period contained the seeds that slowly gave birth to the Renaissance through the confluence of many factors and, thereafter, there were many dramatic and accelerated changes.

First, the crusades were a failure. The second (1148), third (1189), fourth (1198) failed to recapture Jerusalem from the Moslem Saracens. The children's crusade of 1212 ended in disaster. Four more crusades in the 13th century also failed. This had a dramatic impact on European faith. It planted the seeds of doubt and began the process that eventually undermined the spiritual authority of the Papacy.

Second, from 1347 to 1350, the Black Death killed up to one third of the population of Europe. This shook the established order. It redistributed wealth and led to a period of greater prosperity. It also led to an influx of educated immigrants from Constantinople, the center of the Byzantine Holy Roman Empire, into Europe, especially Italy. These immigrants brought with them knowledge of the ancient classical traditions. This influx continued until, finally in 1453, Constantinople fell to the Turks.

Third, various inventions contributed significantly to a changing Europe. In particular, these were the magnetic compass, the clock, gunpowder, and the printing press. Gunpowder came from China to Europe via the Arabs. By 1500, it had altered the nature of war. The medieval castles were no longer strategically important and, as warfare became a question of firepower, the knightly ideals of chivalry became something of the past. In 1450, Gutenberg invented the printing press. From the point of view of the Reformation, it gave more people direct access to the Bible, undermining the need for the authoritarian mediation of the Church. Furthermore, it made possible the production of inexpensive books and stimulated the intellectual community precisely at the time when there was increasing interest in ancient pagan texts.

Petrarch (1304-1374) was another decisive influence in ushering in the Renaissance. As a young man, he fell in love with the classics and decided to dedicate his life to the rediscovery of the cultures of ancient Greece and Rome. By the age of 35, he was one of the most famous literary figures in Europe. With the author Boccaccio, he traveled throughout Europe and to Constantinople in search of ancient texts in monastery libraries. In effect, Petrarch's influence shows us that, although the Church had managed to tame Aristotle, it could not halt the increasing European interest in ancient pagan culture and its more humanistic, Platonic, and non-Christian values. It could not stop the Renaissance.

The Renaissance

The Renaissance was the essential prelude to the birth of the modern era. Within one generation, Columbus discovered the Americas, Leonardo and Michelangelo produced their masterpieces, Luther started the Reformation, and Copernicus claimed that the earth revolved around the sun.

It was no accident that the Renaissance began in small, Italian city-states, such as Florence. In such states, political action was understandable and subject to human will, in contrast to the feudalism that dominated much of the rest of Europe. These states reflected the new value that was being placed on individualism. This new optimistic and self-confident culture developed in an environment of greater wealth and liberty, in which scholars studied the pagan texts of antiquity, painters created sensual works of art, and merchants traded.

In short, medieval monastic ideals were being replaced by new secular values and the rediscovery of the culture of ancient Greece was a vital component in this change. In the 13th century, Aquinas had harnessed Aristotle for the purposes of the Church. However, at this time, few of the works of Plato were known and the vast cultural wealth of pagan ancient Greece remained to be rediscovered. For example, during the Renaissance, the works of the atomists, Epicurus and Lucretius, were rediscovered, and they had a vital influence on the development of science.

However, the humanism of the Renaissance was fueled mainly by the rediscovery of Plato's thought. Marsilio Ficino published the first translation of the complete works of Plato (1470), and his *Platonic Theology* (1482). Neoplatonism became a popular philosophy. In his later works, Plato, under the influence of Pythagoras, had claimed that the universe was essentially mathematical. The Neoplatonists accepted this idea, which also was to be crucial to the development of science.

The work and life of Leonardo da Vinci (1452-1519) portrays the spirit of the Renaissance. His artwork celebrates the human body. He employed careful observations of nature to enhance the beauty of his artistic creations and to advance, in his notebooks, a new scientific spirit, which embraced empiricism, mathematics, mechanics and human creativity. The secret of his knowledge was to 'know how to see.' Leonardo eschewed any divisions in human knowledge, and the nature of his intelligence marks a new humanistic self-consciousness.

Pico della Mirandola (1463-1494) articulated this new self-awareness in his *Oration on the Dignity of Man* (1486), which can be regarded as the manifesto of the Renaissance. Drawing on Plato's creation myth, Mirandola claimed that, when God created humanity, He had no archetypes left and, thus, made Adam free to create his own nature without limits and to determine his own destiny.

These changes were quickly felt throughout Europe. The Renaissance moved north and west. In England, after the long battles of the Wars of the Roses, the new young king Henry VIII gathered around him active intellects, such as Thomas More, the author of *Utopia* (1516). In Holland, More's friend, Erasmus produced a definitive translation of the New Testament (1516) and wrote *In Praise of Folly.*

Finally, the adventurous spirit of the Renaissance produced a generation of explorers and traders. From 1480 on, various Portuguese sailors set out to find gold, which was needed to finance the spice trade with the Arabs, and later to discover a direct route to the Indies around Africa. However, this trade route was unsafe because of Muslim pirates and some explorers began to wonder whether there might be a western route to the Indies. In 1492, Christopher Columbus set out to prove the earth was round and not flat, by trying to reach India from the west. The discovery of the Americas had a huge impact on human optimism. It was a New World waiting to be exploited and later settled. Soon, gold from South America came pouring into Spain. Meanwhile, other explorers helped almost to complete the map of the world. In 1519, Magellan set off to sail around the world with a fleet of ships. Three years later, one ship returned to Spain.

The Reformation

One paradox of the Renaissance was that the new secular spirit spurred the Catholic Church towards new glories, such as the new basilica of St. Peters, the Sistine Chapel, and many other great religious works of art. However, this embracing of the pagan values of the Renaissance by the Church led to its eventual downfall.

Pope Leo X authorized the selling of spiritual indulgences in order to fund the building of St. Peters. While this practice was common earlier, it now reached new depths. It included the remission from sins and release from purgatory, thereby compromising the integrity of the sacrament. While it was this practice that unleashed the fury of Martin Luther, these events were indicative of a much deeper point. As Luther saw it, in embracing the pagan inspired Renaissance, the Church had renounced the anti-Hellenic values of the Bible. In this point we can see the emergence of the Puritanism of some Protestant churches as a rebellion within Christianity against both the authoritarianism of the Catholic Church and the humanism of the Renaissance. In this way, we can appreciate how the Reformation was both libertarian and conservative.

On October 31, 1517, Luther nailed his 95 theses condemning the Catholic establishment to the door of a church in Wittenburg. His work was printed and read widely in Germany, drawing substantial support. Luther asked a fundamental question: How can a person be saved? And he gave an apparently undeniable answer: by his or her individual faith in and relationship with Christ. On this basis, he argued for independence for the individual from religious establishments. By the time Luther was excommunicated in 1520, he had become a furious literary genius and the politically astute leader of a national movement. He soon gave up the idea of reforming the Catholic Church from within, and set up a new church, which led to the proliferation of Protestant Christian sects around northern Europe. In Geneva, John

Calvin articulated a new Protestant theology based on divine predetermination and the depravity of humans after the Fall of Adam. Calvinism claimed that the impossibility of salvation except for the few, who are pre-selected by God. Geneva became the first Protestant theocratic city-state.

With the establishment of national churches apart from Rome, the old political ideal of a unified Christendom was replaced gradually by that of a Europe consisting of independent states. In this way, political power was transferred from the Church to the nation state. This ushered in a period of European wars and a radical rethinking of the nature of political power.

Furthermore, by dissolving the distinction between priest and laity, the Reformation stressed a new idea of individual self-responsibility, which transferred into other aspects of life. The emerging Protestant Churches viewed everyday work and family life as part of a person's religious calling. This provided an alternative to the medieval monastic ideal. The Protestant work ethic also further increased the wealth of an already wealthier Europe. Spanish gold from South America fueled the economies of the north.

The Counter-Reformation

In 1545, the Catholic Church called the first Council of Trent and thereby launched the Counter-Reformation, which initiated a series of institutional changes, including banning the selling of indulgences and compulsory weekly attendance at mass. As intended, these reforms rejuvenated the Church, and this led to the establishment by Ignatius Loyola of a new order, the Jesuits. The Jesuits pioneered a missionary program that took them to all parts of the world. With a view to forming a new Catholic elite in Europe, the Jesuits also transformed education. Jesuit schools taught not only the Catholic faith, but also logic, metaphysics and classical ancient texts. This liberal curriculum had the unintended effect of helping to produce new generations of free thinkers. Galileo, Descartes, Diderot and Voltaire all attended Jesuit schools.

2
The Rise of Science: Copernicus to Galileo

We are accustomed to the idea that we inhabit a miniscule planet that forms a part of a solar system in a huge galaxy, which is only one of billions of galaxies in an expanding material universe. During the medieval period, people had a very different conception of the universe. According to their view, the earth was the flat and still center of the universe. The earth was part of the sublunary world, which is made of the four elements, earth, water, air and fire, each of which had a natural tendency to find its natural place. For this reason, heavy bodies fall and hot gases rise. Above the moon is the celestial or superlunary world, which consists of the stars, which move eternally in circles, and which are made of aether. God exists beyond the celestial realm. The difference between the two views has a deep symbolic and psychological meaning. Instead of being at the center of God's magnificent creation, we are a pinprick in the vastness of space and time. The change also had a huge political and epistemological significance.

Copernicus

The ancient cosmology of Ptolemy was based on the assumption that the earth was still and the planets and sun revolved around it in perfect circles. To make this theory fit the observable facts, Ptolemy's successors had had to postulate increasingly complex epicycles. When the observed movement of a planet was not a perfect circle, another smaller circle, called an epicycle, was postulated to account for the difference. By the time of the Renaissance, Ptolemy's original theory had become very complicated and inelegant. It no longer permitted clear astronomical predictions.

The Church needed a new calendar and thus asked the Polish astronomer and clergyman, Copernicus (1473-1543), to revise Ptolemy's system. Copernicus' investigations led him to the conclusion that further reform of the Ptolemic system was impossible. However, he also found that some ancient Greek thinkers had proposed that the earth revolved around the sun. Because of his Neoplatonic background, Copernicus was convinced that the universe must be governed by simple mathematical laws. Given this, and given the Renaissance spirit of the times, Copernicus took the bold step of working out the detailed implications of this heliocentric hypothesis. In 1514, he published his treatise, *The Little Commentary*, in which he argued that the planets revolved around the sun in the sequence Mercury, Venus, Earth, Mars, Jupiter and Saturn. Later, the pope approved the idea. His main work, *On the Revolutions of Celestial Orbs*, was published a few weeks before his death, with a dedication to the pope. Copernicus was handed a copy of his work on the day of his death.

After his death, the new Gregorian calendar was based on his theory. However, slowly, the emerging Protestant churches began to realize that Copernicus' theory was a fundamental challenge to the authority of scripture. Psalm 93 states: 'The world also is stabilized that it cannot be moved.' Copernicus' view became heresy. As time progressed, the dangerous implications of the theory became more apparent. The Catholic Church began to perceive the theory as a more fundamental threat than even Luther and Calvin.

In fact, they were right. Copernicus' theory was the first step in an intellectual revolution. It began the sharp division between science and philosophy on the one hand, and revealed religion on the other. Copernicus' claim was based on argumentation from empirical evidence rather than authority. At the same time, it became clearer to the Catholic Church that the theory upset the comfortable anthropocentric view of the universe sanctioned by scholastic philosophy. Humans were no longer regarded as the fixed center of God's creation.

Copernicus' theory also reveals another disconcerting and important characteristic of many scientific discoveries, which is that they often contradict appearances. It is not immediately apparent that the earth moves, but Copernicus' amassed evidence to show that it does indeed revolve on its axis and orbit the sun.

Copernicus' revolution unleashed a series of other early scientific discoveries that also threatened the established order. For instance, in 1543, Vesalius' anatomy supplanted that of the ancient Greek Galen,

(130-200 AD), and paved the way for William Harvey's (1578-1657) later theory of the circulation of the blood and Paracelus' chemically based theory of medicine. In particular, Copernicus made possible the discoveries of Galileo in mechanics and those of Kepler in astronomy, and laid the ground for the mechanistic science of Descartes.

Kepler

In fact, Copernicus' observations did not decisively support his conclusion. But those of the later astronomers, Tycho Brahe (1546-1601) and Kepler (1571-1630) did. Brahe built his own observatory and amassed a huge amount of carefully observed mathematical data of the movement of the sun, stars and moon. Kepler moved to Prague from his native Germany to work with Brahe.

When Brahe died, Kepler inherited these mathematical observations. Instead of trying to compile yet more data, Kepler studied Brahe's observations in detail in order to make sense of them. After many false starts, and almost ten years' work, in 1604, Kepler framed the hypothesis that the planets orbit around the sun elliptically, rather than in circles. This is called Kepler's first law. His second law is that each planet moves more rapidly when it is closer to the sun. His third law states that the square of the time of the orbit of a planet around the sun is proportional to the cube root of its mean distance from the sun. This new theory precisely matched the observational evidence.

Influenced by William Gilbert's (1544-1603) work on magnetism and his idea of the earth as a giant magnet (1600), Kepler argued that the planets moved elliptically through the action of a purely mechanical magnetic force.

Kepler was motivated primarily by the Neoplatonic view that the universe must be describable mathematically. By taking the radical step of dropping the assumption that the orbits must be perfect circles, Kepler demonstrated the power of a scientific method that combined careful empirical observation and mathematical description. All the planetary motions could be accurately described and predicted with three simple and precise laws. This was a model.

In 1609, Kepler published his results in *The Harmony of the World.* By this time the Church realized the subversive nature of these results and Kepler's works were placed on the Index of Prohibited Books.

Galileo Galilei

Galileo (1564-1642) was born in Pisa, during the Italian Renaissance, on the very day that Michelangelo died. As a young man, after 'discovering' Euclid's geometry, he studied mechanics and mathematics with passion. At the age of 25, he was appointed Chair of Mathematics at the University of Pisa. In 1592, he moved to the University of Padua and, in 1610, to Florence,

Galileo made four fundamental scientific advances. First, in 1609, he constructed a telescope with a magnification of a thousand, and saw a universe utterly different from anything ever seen before. The sky contained ten times as many stars as are visible to the naked eye. He saw that the Milky Way was a huge cluster of stars, which suggested that the universe was much bigger than had previously been thought. He also observed that there were mountains on the moon and he discovered four of the moons of Jupiter. These observations contradicted the idea that the planetary bodies, like the stars, were just points of light. They no longer appeared to be the eternal celestial bodies of Aristotle's cosmology. The very idea of higher or celestial bodies was under threat. In 1610, Galileo published *The Sidereal Messenger*, which caused a stir in the intellectual society of Europe.

Second, during this period, Galileo observed the phases of the planet Venus, which were explicable only on the assumption that it went around the sun and not the earth. In other words, he provided physical proof of the Copernican system that was independent of Kepler's work. In 1632, Galileo published the *Dialogue concerning the Two Chief World Systems-Ptolemaic and Copernican,* in which he argued that the earth revolves around the sun.

In 1600, the Catholic Church had burned at the stake the philosopher Giodarno Bruno for his heretical views. After a long period of inquisition starting in 1615, and after some hesitation, in 1633, Galileo was found guilty of heresy and disobedience to the Church for treating Copernicus' claims as a proven fact. Galileo was imprisoned. He was forced to recant. This, however, spelled defeat for the Church. It lost the moral claim to represent the human search for knowledge, and these events opened a chasm between science and religion.

Third, Aristotle's physics was based on the perceived qualities of objects and on verbal explanations. In opposition to his Aristotelian colleagues, and influenced by the atomism of the rediscovered ancient philosopher Lucretius, Galileo proposed that investigations of nature should be based only on measurable qualities, such as weight, motion, number, size and shape. Scientific results should be numerical. Furthermore, these mathematical observations should result in mathematically precise laws. Indeed, Galileo claimed that 'the Book of Nature is written in mathematical characters.'

As Galileo himself saw, this view has some very dramatic implications. It means that non-mathematical perceptual or secondary qualities, such as color, must be explicable in terms of the mathematical or primary properties of matter, such as motion, weight, size and shape. It implies that all things differ only in such quantitative ways. Thus, Aristotle's four basic elements, earth, water, air and fire should be replaced with the single idea of matter, which has those primary qualities to different degrees. It also implies that this matter is inert. Material things do not have inherent purposes or natural tendencies that explain their actions, This paved the way for Descartes' claim that all physical changes should be explained mechanically.

Fourth, in accordance with these ideas, Galileo developed the science of mechanics. Aristotle had argued that heavier bodies fall faster than lighter ones because earthly bodies have a natural tendency to find their proper position in the scheme of things. There is a famous, but probably false, story that Galileo publicly refuted Aristotle's claim by dropping two bodies of unequal weight from the leaning tower of Pisa, which fell with equal speed. In fact, by employing mathematical analysis to repeated experiments on bodies rolling down inclines, Galileo showed that their motion was independent of their weight. In this way, he formulated the first version of the principle of inertia, a notion vital to the future of physics. The principle of inertia implies that a body moving in vacuum will continue its movement indefinitely, unless acted on by some resisting force. In other words, force is required to bring about changes in velocity, rather than merely to maintain existing motion, as Aristotle had claimed. In 1638, Galileo published the *Discourse concerning Two New Sciences*, which contains an initial statement of the principle of inertia, later refined and extended by Descartes and Newton.

In summary, with these four advances, Galileo overturned the dominance of traditional Aristotelian physics. Furthermore, the events surrounding his condemnation opened a deep divide between religion and science. Although most intellectuals, including new generations of scientists, remained Christian, there was a growing perceived need to rethink the view of the universe and the nature of knowledge.

Some Other Scientists

However, Galileo left physics with a problem. Unaware of the importance of Kepler's work, he had assumed that the planets orbit around the sun in circles, and he had mistakenly thought that their circular orbits could be explained in terms of inertia. However, as

Descartes saw, the principle of inertia applies only to uniform motion in a straight line. Thus, how could the elliptical orbits of the planets be explained? Descartes tried to answer this question but, in fact, Newton gave a more definitive answer with his theory of gravity, first conceived after 1666.

Galileo was the most important member of a generation of other scientists with similar ideas. Gassendi measured the speed of sound, and developed a primitive molecular theory of heat. In 1636, his friend Mersenne did other work on the physics of sound using vibrating strings In 1611, Kepler studied the refraction of light by lenses, and, in 1621, Snell formulated the mathematically precise laws of refraction, which enabled the construction of better lenses. Gilbert's earlier work on magnetism spurred others to study the actions of magnets.

Descartes stands out as another giant in this new generation of scientists. By employing his geometrical conception of matter, he tried to unify the work of others, as well as his own experiments, into one overall theory of mechanical physics, which covered areas as diverse as the formation and movement of the planets, heat, light, magnetism, anatomy and animal behavior. He also tried to give this new conception of science a firm philosophical basis.

The Philosophical Quest

These new challenges to the scholastic tradition of the Catholic Church opened a philosophical debate primarily about the nature of evidence and explanation. The first philosophers to see this clearly were Bacon, Hobbes and, especially, Descartes. As advocates of the new sciences, the early modern philosophers had to argue for a new conception of knowledge and explanation and, at the same time, define the metaphysical and theological implications of their views.

1) Evidence: Up to the late 16th century, a common form of scholarly argument was to amass relevant quotations from authoritative sources, such as the texts of Aristotle, Aquinas, and the Bible. Investigation consisted in studying these texts, and debate often consisted in citing and making deductions from them. However, the emerging new sciences, such as astronomy, had little place for arguments from authority. They relied mostly on observation and mathematical reasoning. The English philosopher Francis Bacon argued strongly against authority based arguments. The new science required freedom from such authority to investigate the universe without prejudice and superstition.

2) Explanation: Traditionally, medieval thinkers tried to explain natural events, such as the motion of planets, in terms of natural and divine purposes. Viewed in this way, nature becomes the handiwork of God. Early modern philosophers, such as Descartes and Bacon, argued that final causes could not be used in the scientific study of matter. They replaced explanation by purposes with mechanistic explanation by physical causal laws. Additionally, medieval tradition had conceived of the universe as a hierarchical organic whole, with different levels of being. Between the macrocosmic universe and the microcosm man, there existed affinities or correspondences. Accordingly, the natural world could be understood as analogous to a living organism.

Furthermore, in the Aristotelian scholastic view, the physical world consists of four basic elements, earth, water, air and fire, each of which has a natural tendency to seek its proper position in the scheme of things. Earthly things fall and hot things rise because of their natures. In contrast, Galileo and Descartes attempted to quantify nature. According to them, the study of nature should concern itself exclusively with the measurable properties of matter, such as size, shape and motion. This puts all natural things on the same level, subject to the same physical laws. It eliminates the need for Aristotle's four elements and for his inherent purposes in nature. It means that things differ only in quantitative ways and that explanation must be mechanical.

This whole conflict had very high stakes: the nature of the universe and of human life. According to the medieval Christian view, the universe was a quasi-organic piece of handiwork created by God, full of omens and signs. Modern science was beginning to paint an entirely different picture. It seemed to portray the universe as completely material, and all changes as mechanical. Such a view apparently left no place for the soul or for God, and thus threatened to make religion peripheral. On the other hand, the optimism of the new science promised much. By understanding nature scientifically, humankind will be able to improve its lot. By understanding ourselves, we will become freer.

Descartes framed the fundamental questions of this age of transformation. Few thinkers of the time argued for a wholesale rejection of religious thought. So, how could the new science be reconciled with religion? Because the two world-views clashed, and with so much at stake, thinkers had to question the nature of knowledge itself. Descartes pioneered this philosophical reflection. He wrote: 'No more useful inquiry can be proposed than that which seeks to determine the nature and scope of human knowledge' (AT X 397). Descartes saw the need to re-evaluate the basis of knowledge in order to reconcile the new science with religion.

3

Bacon and the New Map of Knowledge

Sir Francis Bacon (1561-1626) was a politician and a philosopher, not a major scientist. But while Galileo was studying motion and the planets in Italy, in England Bacon was independently developing a new vision of knowledge. Inspired by the discovery of America and the new age of exploration, he envisioned a new continent of scientific knowledge for which he would provide the map. This consisted of three elements: a classification of knowledge, a new scientific method to free the mind of its prejudices and a utopian vision of the power and meaning of knowledge.

1) Utopian Vision

According to Bacon, knowledge should be used to gain power and control over nature for the benefit and liberation of humanity. This was humanity's new spiritual mission, the worldly counterpart of spiritual salvation. Bacon felt that he was articulating the principles for the dawn of a new era. However, this required sweeping aside the Scholastic view of knowledge, which dominated European learning and had become stagnant.

2) Classification of Knowledge

Bacon outlined a plan for a complete system of knowledge, which can be divided into four parts. The first part of the plan is the classification of knowledge, which is found in the *Advancement of Learning.*

3) The New Method

The second part of the plan is found in the *Novum Organon*, where Bacon sets out the methodology for scientific learning, which he calls the new method of induction, and where he catalogues the prejudices of the mind that interfere with its employment.

A Political Life

Bacon studied at Cambridge University, and later practiced law as a barrister. Aged 23, he became a member of the English Parliament. Hungry for power, Bacon was unable to advance his political career during the reign of Elizabeth I. After her death in 1603, Bacon's political ambitions were rekindled. He enjoyed the support of King James' favorite, the Duke of Buckingham. He was appointed Solicitor General in 1613; Attorney General in 1616; and member of the Privy Council in 1617. Finally, in 1618, Bacon was appointed Lord Chancellor of England, the highest legal position in the country after that of the King. In 1621, he was given the title Viscount of St. Albans. However, later that year, he was found guilty of accepting bribes, and he lost all political power. This verdict was in part the result of a failed political intrigue. After the guilty verdict, Bacon was imprisoned in the Tower of London but only for a few days. However, he was banished from the court and was forced to sell his London mansion to Buckingham.

During the lulls in his political career, Bacon engaged in philosophy. His first work, the *Essays,* appeared in 1597 and his first book t*he Advancement of Learning* was published in 1605. In 1610, he wrote *New Atlantis* concerning the social or co-operative nature of scientific research. *Novum Organum* was published in 1620. After his impeachment, Bacon retired from public life, but he continued to write. He wrote two works on natural history: *Historia Ventorum*, 1622 and *Historia Vitae et Mortis*, 1623.

1) Utopian Vision

Bacon's work does not argue for a systematic philosophical theory. Rather it consists of a vision. He sees the urgent need to advance learning through experimental science in order to bring great benefits to humanity. His whole thought is dedicated to finding the means to bring about this vision. He enters into philosophical debates only insofar as it is necessary for this end, and he evaluates systems of thought in terms of this end. Most of his work is pragmatic. Much of the *Advancement of Learning* consists of a call to action. He advocates more universities and libraries, as well as the establishment of laboratories, museums of technology, centers of investigation, biological gardens, and collaborative international research projects. Many of his suggestions are very innovative. For example, he calls for clinical records, basic work in preventive medicine and the social sciences. He campaigns for fundamental reforms in education. His writing is both enthusiastic and full of worldly wisdom. In short, he writes as a politician close to power with a philosophical vision. This was a new way to practice philosophy and the force of his vision is not dissipated by metaphysical considerations.

Bacon sets out his pragmatic program in *The Great Instauration* (or the Great Reform) at the beginning of the *Novum Organum.* First, the program requires the classification of all knowledge. Second, it requires the elaboration of a new scientific method. Third, it necessitates a natural history of all phenomena in the universe, which employs the new scientific method. Fourth, it requires the development of a new philosophy based on these other investigations. Bacon does not envisage himself carrying out all these aims. He calls on others to join in the task. He himself works out the first two parts in the *Advancement of Learning* and *Novum Organum*, and towards the end of his life he began work on the third part. However, because his work captured the new spirit of the times, his clarion call was heard around Europe. In a way, despite the deep philosophy differences, Descartes' work can be seen as a continuation of the third and fourth parts of Bacon's program. Descartes unifies the sciences and builds a new systematic philosophy, much as Bacon had intended.

2) The Classification of Knowledge

In 1592, Bacon wrote 'I have taken all knowledge for my province.' To advance his vision, Bacon attempts to draw a detailed map of this territory. In other words, he tries to classify all knowledge. He thought that such a classification was necessary in order to determine the kinds of methods and problems appropriate to each kind of inquiry.

His classification, which is contained in the second part of the *Advancement*, is based on the three faculties, reason, memory, and imagination. Correspondingly, there are three forms of knowledge: science or philosophy, history, and poetry. History should be distinguished from science because of its concern with particular rather than general truths.

Bacon divides the field of philosophy or science into two parts: natural philosophy and rational theology, i.e. the attempt to prove the existence of God. Natural philosophy is divided into the theoretical and the practical. The first is the scientific inquiry into causes. The second is the inquiry into the production of effects. Natural science, the inquiry into causes, is further divided into physics, which deals with efficient and material causes, and metaphysics, concerned with formal and final causes. Final causes seek to explain natural phenomena by citing the purpose for which they were created. Bacon does not deny final causes; however, he rejects the idea that they are a part of science. Science is directed towards discovering the form of things, such as the form of heat or of gold. A form is a state or configuration of matter.

Perhaps the main aim of Bacon's classification of knowledge is to separate revealed theology and the empirical advancement of the sciences. Given his vision and given the fact that European institutions of learning were dominated by Scholastic theology, Bacon sees an urgent need to assign Scholasticism and speculation to its proper place.

3) Toward a Method

The main aim of Bacon's philosophy was to extend knowledge so that humankind could control the forces of nature through scientific experiments and discoveries. This requires developing a scientific methodology. Bacon develops this methodology in three stages. First, he argues against mistaken approaches to learning and, in particular Scholasticism. Second, he tries to catalogue the kinds of prejudices that humans have when investigating, which he calls the idols of the mind. Third, he advances a positive theory of science based on the new method of induction and his theory of forms.

a) The Criticism of False Learning

In the first part of the *Advancement of Learning,* Bacon tries to remove obstacles to the methodological progress of science by criticizing three unsatisfactory schools of learning.

1) The most influential of these was the Aristotelian Scholasticism, which he calls the 'disputatious' style of learning, which fruitlessly speculates about theology. To reject Scholasticism, Bacon first sharply separates philosophy from theology, which Scholasticism confuses. Bacon does not reject religious knowledge, but argues that it must be divinely revealed and thus is not the proper province of philosophy. Nothing about God's nature can be known scientifically or through reasoning. In contrast, the knowledge of the natural world must be acquired through observation and reason. Also, Bacon criticizes Scholasticism for over-emphasis on deduction, which cannot yield new knowledge, and for too little emphasis on observation, which can. In this way, most scholastic philosophers aim to preserve tradition, rather than seeking new knowledge.

2) Bacon also criticizes the humanism of the Renaissance, which he calls the 'delicate' style of learning. He rebukes it for indifference to the serious business of science and for too much preoccupation with vacuous eloquence and polite morality.

3) The third defective style of learning is that of the occultists, such as astrology or what we might call today pseudo-sciences. Despite their desire to master nature, the occultists uncritically accept myths and fables. By contrast, scientific knowledge should be based on rational procedure and observation that anyone could critically accept.

b) The Idols of the Mind

To reinforce these critiques, Bacon catalogues common forms of prejudice that must be overcome for knowledge to progress. These are the idols of the mind, presented in the first book of the *Novum Organon*. There are four kinds of idols.

1) The idols of the tribe are intellectual weaknesses generally inherent in human nature. These include the disposition of the mind to be misled by the errors and dullness of the senses. We ignore the invisible changes in nature that can explain observable changes. With

the aid of instruments and careful systematic observation, we can correct these defects because 'the senses suffice for knowledge.'

2) The idols of the cave or den are personal prejudices and biases. For example, some people are obsessed by details, others by the whole, and some people tend to look for differences, others for similarities.

3) The idols of the marketplace are those tendencies to error due to the bewitchment of the mind by language. 'Words are but the images of matter,' and we should not suppose that they reflect things truly. Words can be vague, confused, and badly defined.

4) The idols of the theatre are the accepted but mistaken schools of philosophy, which were discussed earlier.

c) The New Method of Induction

More positively, Bacon advances a method for the new sciences, which he calls the method of eliminative induction, and which is to be contrasted with simple enumerative induction. In enumerative induction, we derive an unrestricted general conclusion from an observed finite set of singular cases. From the fact that we have seen a few white swans, we rashly conclude that all swans are white. In contrast, the scientist should look for counter-instances to falsify a hypothesis, which can be eliminated. The method should be eliminative and not enumerative.

Bacon gives a detailed example of his method at work in the discovery of the nature of heat. First, we draw up three lists: a list of hot things that are otherwise unalike; a list of cold things, which are otherwise like the hot things; and finally, a list of things of varying degrees of heat. By carefully comparing these tables, we can reject some suggestions as to the nature of heat and make a first affirmation as to its nature. From a number of such affirmations of the lowest degree of generality, we can suggest laws that are slightly more general and so on. Any suggested law or hypothesis should be tested in new circumstances. We must try to prove it false and, if we cannot, the hypothesis is to that extent confirmed. In particular, we should look for experiments that hasten the process of induction by allowing us to reject false hypotheses quickly. For example, Bacon mentioned 'prerogative instances,' which separate the characteristics both found in hot bodies. By systematically applying this method, Bacon says we conclude that heat is the rapid irregular motion of the small parts of bodies.

Bacon contrasts his method with that of the Scholastics. On the one hand, Bacon's method begins from the observation of particulars and, by eliminative induction, builds systematically to more general conclusions. On the other hand, the Scholastic method involves reasoning deductively from the general to the particular. This deductive method cannot result in any advancement in knowledge. It consists in applying old knowledge to new cases and is essentially conservative.

The Theory of Forms

Bacon supplements his method of induction with a claim about the aim of science. Science should be the investigation of 'the form of a simple nature.' The form is identical with the simple nature. For instance, the form of heat is both a necessary and sufficient condition of heat. The form of heat is always present in hot things, absent in cold things, and varies in correspondence with the degree of heat. Forms are configurations of matter. Bacon thinks we should explain observable properties or 'simple natures' in terms of the fine structure of matter. The form of gold is that arrangements of matter which constitutes gold.

4

Descartes: The Unity of Science

As a young man, Renée Descartes (1596–1650) was rather lost. He had no real direction in his life and he felt unhappy with his scholastic education without really knowing why. However, these problems were answered by a series of events that gave Descartes a vision and a life project, through which he became a great and famous scientist and philosopher. In effect, he became the first spokesman for the new modern period. In this way, Descartes philosophical quest is intimately bound up with the story of his life.

Biography

Descartes was born in France and raised as a Catholic by his grandmother. His mother died while he was a baby and his father moved away and remarried. After his grandmother died in 1610, Descartes had little contact with his family, except his sister. At the age of ten, he was sent to a prestigious and traditional Jesuit boarding school, which he disliked. Afterwards, he studied law at the University of Poitiers.

However, Descartes was undecided about his career. In 1618, he joined the army in the Netherlands, as a gentleman soldier. He was idle and unhappy 'in the midst of turmoil and uneducated soldiers.' Later that year, he met Isaac Beeckman. They discovered a shared interest in mathematics, and Beckman became Descartes' mentor. Through serious study, the young Descartes acquired a proficiency in mathematics, and this was to change his life.

On the 10th November 1619, in Bavaria, Descartes had a series of visions. To escape the cold, he had shut himself in a small stove-heated room. During the day, after meditating and thinking deeply, he had a revelation of the unity of the sciences according to a few basic geometrical principles, which would make the sciences 'no harder to grasp than the series of numbers.' That night he had three dreams, in one of which he saw an encyclopedia that represented the sciences unified. According to Descartes, his visions were divinely revealed and, from this, he concluded that his future work in science could not conflict with the basic doctrines of the Church. He noted that, on this day, he had discovered 'the fundamental principles of a wonderful discovery.' To appreciate the significance of this revelation, remember that, in Descartes' time, the subjects of astronomy, mechanics, optics, chemistry, physiology and medicine were considered as separate disciplines. Descartes saw that they could be unified as one subject, physics, by a few mechanical explanatory principles. This event marks the beginning of Descartes' work as a philosopher and scientist.

After his dreams, Descartes started working seriously on *The Rules for the Direction of the Mind*, in which he tried to employ the methods of arithmetic and geometry as a model for all investigation and problem solving. Later he claimed that, by strictly applying his own method, 'I became very adept at unraveling all the questions' of geometry and arithmetic.

In 1625, he moved to Paris where he became a friend of the mathematician Mersenne. Around this time, Descartes became interested in optics and discovered the law of refraction. However, his busy social life prevented him from working seriously and, in 1629, he moved to Holland, where preferred the comparative quiet and seclusion.

By now, Descartes' interest in mathematics was waning. He had conceived a new, more ambitious project, which was to become his classic *The World*, a pioneering work in physics. This was a busy period. He conducted philosophical discussions by letter, and he experimented in optics and physiology. *The World* contains chapters on heat, light, weight, the formation of the planets, the nature of comets, the formation of the earth, the tides, the laws of nature, and a treatise on physiology. By seeking the unifying principles behind all of these natural phenomena, Descartes aimed to make the workings of nature clear. This involved uncovering the basic mechanisms that govern matter. In brief, he claimed that material things are made of atom-like corpuscles and that all physical reactions can be explained in terms of the motion of these corpuscles. This is the basic mechanism that underlies all perceived changes. In 1633, shortly before *The World* was due to be published, Descartes heard of Galileo's condemnation by the Church and he suppressed his own work.

This event marks another turning point in Descartes' life. In the period after Galileo's condemnation, Descartes perceived an urgent need to provide a metaphysical basis for his natural philosophy. He started working on the *Discourse on a Method.* By the time the *Discourse* was published in 1637, Descartes was married and had a young daughter Francine. This was the happiest period of his life. He cultivated a herb garden, dissected animals and gave accounts of the workings and physics of various simple machines such as the pulley, the lever, the cog wheel. In 1638, he started work on *the Meditations on First Philosophy*, his major work, which contains 'the entire foundation' for his physics. Descartes' period of personal happiness ended suddenly in 1640, when Francine died of fever. Descartes said that her death was 'the greatest sorrow' that he had experienced in his life.

The Vision, Aims and Strategy

Descartes' vision of a unified physical theory of the world based on geometry required a philosophical basis because, otherwise, Scholasticism would continue to dominate European thought. Like Bacon, he appreciated that modern science challenged the scholastic idea of knowledge based on authority.

His philosophical quest, as advanced in the *Meditations*, consists of two basic aims. First, in order to argue against the scholastic view of the world and knowledge, Descartes provides a philosophical foundation for his physics. Second, he attempts to prove that his physics is compatible with the basic doctrines of the Christian religion, despite appearances to the contrary. To achieve this second aim, he argues that modern physics requires the existence of God and that a proper understanding of matter as an inert substance will demonstrate the existence of the soul as something distinct from the body.

The Three-fold Strategy

To achieve his two overall aims, Descartes has a brilliantly simple argumentative strategy. He tries to show that the only way to answer radical skepticism is with a philosophy that provides a solid foundation, at the same time, for both his own physics and for the essentials of the Christian religion. In effect, he argues that Scholasticism and materialistic atheism are both bankrupt because neither can answer radical skepticism.

Given his overall aims and this strategy, we can divide the *Meditations* into three sections.

a) In the first section, he demonstrates that skepticism needs to be answered. In other words, Descartes draws our attention to a new philosophical problem, namely that it is reasonable to doubt even the claim that the external world consists of material objects. In other words, in the first Meditation, he argues that radical skepticism is reasonable to the extent that it requires an answer. This is a politically subversive argument because it directly undermines the very idea of knowledge based on authority.

b) In the second section, he refutes this radical skepticism by arguing that clear and distinct ideas are true. Furthermore, this conclusion also enables Descartes to argue against Scholasticism and in favor of his own physics, which, unlike Scholasticism, consists of clear and distinct mathematical ideas. In this way, he provides a foundation for modern science as opposed to scholastic philosophy, which cannot answer radical skepticism.

How does Descartes argue for his conclusion that clear and distinct ideas are true? Now, we shall see the brilliance of his general strategy. He does so with the following argument:

1. If God exists, then clear and distinct ideas are true.
2. <u>God exists</u>.
3. Therefore, clear and distinct ideas are true.

Descartes provides independent arguments for both of the above premises. In this way, he not only answers skepticism, but also at the same time shows that both atheism and Scholasticism are mistaken and, furthermore, that they cannot solve the real skeptical problem presented in the first Meditation. This line of argument is pursued in Meditations 3 and 5.

c) The third section consists of another line of argument, which is designed to prove that the soul must be a substance distinct from matter. Once again, Descartes' argumentative strategy is brilliant. He argues that this conclusion directly follows from points that he has already established. First, as we shall see, it is implied by the very nature of doubt. Second, he argues that, given his modern geometric and anti-scholastic view of matter, the essence of the mind and that of matter are necessarily different and that, therefore, the soul and the body are distinct. This line of argument is pursued in Meditations 2 and 6.

It is very important to bear in mind Descartes' overall aims and his strategy when we examine the details of the arguments. To summarize, first, he first shows that there is a real skeptical problem. Second, he solves that problem by proving that clear and distinct ideas are true by demonstrating the existence of God. In this way, he shows that his physics has a solid foundation and that this requires, and therefore is compatible with, the existence of God. Third, he argues that a proper scientific understanding of matter reveals that the soul and body are distinct. In short, physics and religion are secure, but Scholasticism is left without foundations.

1) Reasonable Doubt

In the first Meditation, Descartes presents his method of doubt. He calls it a method in part because it is a philosophical exercise or training that frees us from the prejudice that the world is how we perceive it to be. By practicing the art of doubting, we will become accustomed to assenting only to clear and distinct ideas, and this is the key to Descartes' whole method. Doubt does not imply thinking that our beliefs are false. It means suspending judgment as to their truth. In effect, Descartes' method of doubt amounts to withholding the judgment that anything in the external world corresponds to our ideas in the mind. Furthermore, Descartes claims that knowledge requires certainty, which we can gain only by rejecting the uncertain. Hence, doubt is an important tool for gaining secure knowledge.

The main part of the first Meditation consists of three arguments, each designed to prove that radical doubt is reasonable. However, the first two are false starts, and it is only given the success of the third argument that they have any force.

1) The First Stage

Descartes notes that many of his beliefs are derived from sense perception, which has deceived him in the past. He argues that it is foolish to trust something known to deceive us, and concludes that we should not trust beliefs based on the senses. However, Descartes claims that this first argument does not support a universal doubt. For example, on the basis of it, he cannot reasonably doubt that he has a body. Such doubts require a more radical argument.

2) The Second Stage

Descartes recalls that lucid dreams can be indistinguishable from waking experience. Thus, there are no certain internal criteria to tell whether one is awake or merely dreaming and, any given experience could be a dream. However, once again, Descartes notes that this second argument does not legitimize a universal doubt. For example, it does not legitimize doubting that the simple ideas that compose our dreams (such as shape and size) are real.

3) The Third Stage

In the third stage, Descartes claims that he has no evidence against the claim that there is a supremely powerful and intelligent spirit, which does its utmost to deceive him. However, if there were a powerful deceiving demon, he would be mistaken even in thinking that his sense experiences correspond to external objects at all. The argument is as follows:

Argument A

1 I have no evidence that there is no powerful spirit deceiving me.
2 If there were such a demon, then all my beliefs would be mistaken.
3 If I have no evidence against the claim that a belief is mistaken <u>then that belief is open to reasonable doubt.</u>
4 Therefore, all my beliefs are open to reasonable doubt

To understand the crucial first premise, consider the following two theories, A and B:

A. The ideas that I now have are caused by material objects
B. The ideas that I now have are caused by a deceiving demon.

Premise 1 claims that there is no evidence to show that theory A is more likely to be true than theory B. The two theories explain equally well the empirical data, namely the sensory ideas that I am now having. Hence, there is no good reason for thinking that any one of the two theories is more likely to be true.

This point forces us to make a sharp distinction between an idea perceived and the external cause of that idea. We can appreciate this distinction by considering two questions. First, can you imagine an experience exactly like the one that you are having now, except that it is not caused by external objects? We seem to be forced to answer 'Yes' because the cause of the perception lies outside the perception itself. Second, do you have any evidence that your current experience is not in fact the duplicate? We seem forced to answer 'No' because we have admitted that the original and duplicate experiences are exactly alike. Therefore, radical doubt is reasonable.

Remember that this skeptical argument is aimed to present a challenge, which requires the reconstruction of knowledge on a secure rational foundation. Therefore, according to Descartes, radical doubt is reasonable, but it must and can be answered. He is not a skeptic.

2) The First Line of Argument: Clear and Distinct Ideas

After the first Meditation, Descartes' work follows two tracks. Along the first, he tries to establish the existence of the physical world by proving the existence of God. Along the second, Descartes reveals the nature of the mind, and its separation from the body.

To return to the first track, Descartes must bridge the gap from knowledge of his own mind or ideas to that of the external world. Until he does so, he cannot claim any knowledge concerning the external world. Descartes' strategy for bridging the knowledge-gap between experience and the world consists of two steps. In the first step, Descartes tries to establish that if God exists, then he can treat his own faculties of judgment as reliable and be sure that clear and distinct ideas are true. In the second, he tries to prove the existence of God. The two steps can be represented with the following argument.

Argument B

1 If God exists then clear and distinct ideas are true.
2 God exists.
3 Therefore clear and distinct ideas are true.

In the above argument, the first premise is justified because God is a perfect being, and therefore, He is not a deceiver. Thus, we can be sure that our clear and distinct ideas are true if God exists. The principle that clear and distinct ideas are true serves as a bridge between the realm of private ideas and the external world because it establishes what the external world is like solely on the basis of how ideas seem to the subject. If an idea is clear and distinct, then I can know that it is so while I am having the idea.

To show that the second premise is true, Descartes presents two arguments for the existence of God. Both start from the premise that he, Descartes, has an idea of God. To show that he does indeed have such an idea, he argues that, because he doubts, he is imperfect. From this, he concludes that he also has the idea of absolute perfection and hence, the idea of God.

a) The Causal Argument

In the Third Meditation, Descartes argues that God is the only possible cause of the idea of God. The hinge of this argument is the Principle of Adequate Reality, which claims that there must be at least as much reality in the total cause as in the effect. This principle is required by the Principle of Sufficient Reason because if the cause had less reality than the effect, then the surplus reality in the effect would be without a cause.

What are degrees of reality? There are three levels of being: the first consists of properties, such as being green; the second, finite substances, such as horses; and the third, infinite substances. To prove that God exists, Descartes applies the Principle of Adequate Reality to the content of his ideas or what ideas represent. Every idea must have a cause equal in reality to what it is an idea of. If A has a lesser degree of reality than B, then an idea of B cannot have been caused by A. Consequently, only God himself has a sufficient degree of reality to cause the idea of God. We can summarize Descartes' first argument as follows:

Argument C

1 I have an idea of God.
2 This idea must have a cause.
3 There cannot be less reality in the cause than in the effect.
4 If my idea of God were caused by anything other than God, then <u>there would be less reality in the cause than in the effect.</u>
5 Therefore, God exists

b) The Ontological Argument

In the Fifth Meditation, Descartes offers a simple proof for the existence of God based on the nature of His essence. The essence of a thing consists in its essential properties. Descartes argues that the essence of God involves His existence. God is a being with every perfection (or good quality) and, according to Descartes, existence is a perfect quality. If God did not exist then He would lack a perfect quality, which is impossible.

Conclusion

Through argument B, Descartes thinks that he has proved the principle that clear and distinct ideas are true. In this way, by the Sixth Meditation, Descartes has restored his knowledge of the world and has answered the skepticism of the First Meditation.

From his search, he has learned three very important lessons, central to his major aims. First, he has learned that sense experience on its own is not a reliable way to gain knowledge. It has to be vindicated by reason.

Second, the principle that clear and distinct ideas are true furnishes us with a way of avoiding error; we should suspend our assent to ideas that are unclear and indistinct. This is a vitally important result for Descartes' physics. Matter should be described only with the clear and distinct ideas of mathematics. In other words, science should concern itself only with the measurable properties of matter, such as size, shape, and motion, which constitute the essence of matter. This is the only way to avoid error and skepticism. In contrast, the principle that clear and distinct ideas are true also shows that the unclear, non-mathematical ideas of Scholasticism should not be accepted.

Third, argument B shows how the new science can be reconciled with religion. The scientific study of nature must be grounded in clear methodological principles, which require us to show that God exists. Science requires the existence of God. Otherwise, radical skepticism could not be defeated.

3) The Second Line of Argument: Mind and Matter

The third section of the *Meditations* consists of a long line of argumentation to prove that the mind or soul is distinct from the material body. It has three phases. In the first, Descartes shows what the essence of the mind is. In the second, he describes the essence of matter. Finally, he argues that the two must be distinct substances. The significance of this argument is that, according to Descartes, a proper understanding of matter shows us that the soul is something distinct from matter. He sees this as a theological advantage of doing physics properly. Once again, physics must be compatible with religion.

The Essence of the Mind

After showing in the First Meditation that radical skepticism is a problem, in the Second Meditation, Descartes contends that such skepticism cannot extend to the mind. He does so with the famous argument of the Cogito: 'I think; therefore I am.' The point of the argument is that even a malicious demon could not deceive me into believing that I do not exist. Even if a demon were attempting to deceive me about this, I still cannot doubt that I exist, for, I have to exist in order to be deceived. Consequently, even the possibility of a deceiving demon cannot be a reason for doubting my own existence. I doubt; therefore, I am. Therefore, I cannot doubt that I am.

To better appreciate this argument, let us put it into the context of the text. In the Second Meditation, even after the Cogito. Descartes cannot be sure of very much. For example, he cannot be certain that he has a body, because, at this stage, the existence of external objects is still in doubt. For this reason, the argument of the Cogito is specifically 'I think; therefore I am,' rather than, say, 'I walk; therefore I am.' The premise of the argument has to be certain, and Descartes claims that, even at this stage, he can be certain that he thinks, but not that he walks.

This point reveals a vital clue about the nature of the mind. My conscious mental states seem to disclose themselves to me in such a way that I cannot be mistaken about them while I am having them. If I believe that I am thinking, then I am thinking. This is why the premise of the Cogito (i.e. 'I think') is indubitable. For Descartes, the word 'thought' indicates a range of conscious mental states such that the person who experiences them is immediately aware of them. The word stands for any conscious mental state, such as doubting, willing, feeling and imagining. In today's terminology, Descartes claims that conscious mental states are both evident and incorrigible. They are evident because if I am thinking p, then I must know that I am. I cannot be ignorant about it. They are incorrigible because if I believe that I am thinking p, then it is true that I am thinking p. I cannot be mistaken about it.

Descartes defines ideas as the immediate object of perception. This is a subjective and essentially private definition of mental states. Pain is pain because of the way it feels to the person undergoing it. In other words, according to Descartes, the content of mental states or ideas should be defined by how they are perceived by the person who has them. We may call this an introspective account of the content of mental states, because it affirms that we should define mental states by their introspective feel, rather than by their causal role or their potential effects on behavior.

Having proved that he exists, Descartes' next step is to establish what his essence is. The essence of something is the properties that the thing must have to be and remain what it is. In the Second Meditation, Descartes claims that his essence is to think. This constitutes the essence of the mind: the having of ideas as characterized above.

In the Sixth Meditation, he argues for the stronger claim that the whole of his essence is to think. His only essential attribute is thought. The mind has one and only one essential property or attribute. This means that all properties of the mind are simply modes or modifications of its essential attribute, thought. All properties of the mind are only different types of thought.

The Essence of Matter

In the Sixth Meditation, Descartes tries to characterize the essence of matter. He claims that the whole essence of matter consists in its being extended in space, or in such properties as shape, size and motion. This assertion links back to the very first track of argumentation mentioned earlier. We can understand material objects clearly and distinctly only when we grasp them under the geometrical properties of extension. This ensures the science of matter can and should consist in quantifiable laws. In claiming that matter is extension, Descartes supports his mathematical view of science and ensures that the sciences consist of methodologically sound distinct and clear ideas.

To show that the essence of matter is extension, Descartes argues that a body can lose any of its properties, except extension without ceasing to be a material body. The essence of a thing consists in the properties without which that thing would cease to exist. Descartes claims that a body can lose hardness, weight, color and heat without ceasing to be a body. Since it cannot lose extension, extension is the essential attribute of material bodies.

This suggests that all physical changes should be explained solely in terms of extension, or as the result of matter in motion. This was a revolutionary thesis. Scholastic philosophers tended to explain natural changes in terms of final causes or natural purposes. Descartes complains that this amounts to the attribution of 'a tiny mind' to inanimate bodies. For example, the Scholastics think of the heaviness of a body as something mental, akin to a desire to reach the center of the earth. This is how they explain why bodies fall. In other words, Scholasticism projects mental ideas into the material world.

In sharp contrast, Descartes argues that all physical changes can be explained mechanically, in terms of the motion of atom-like corpuscles. Since all matter is of the same kind and is governed by the same laws, the differing reactions of bodies must be explained in terms of the differing size, shape and motion of the corpuscles that make them up. For this reason, Descartes thinks that, with a few simple principles of motion, we can explain all natural phenomena.

This point underlies Descartes' initial grand vision of the unity of the physical sciences. Optics, mechanics, magnetism, astronomy, and physiology should not be conceived as separate subjects. Such an view prevents one from looking for general explanatory principles. Given the uniform nature of matter and of the laws governing it, the sciences should be unified.

Descartes' conception of matter as extension has some radical consequences. First, it implies that a vacuum is impossible. Matter as extension and physical space are identical, and hence, there can be no empty space. Secondly, his conception of matter also implies that there are no indivisible atoms. All parts of matter must be extended and anything that is extended is, like space, infinitely divisible. Although Descartes employs the idea of corpuscles, strictly speaking he is not an atomist. Thirdly, Descartes holds that all properties of matter must be explained in terms of matter in motion. But since there is no vacuum for bodies to move into, 'the only possible movement of bodies is in a circle.' As one part of matter moves, it pushes another out of the place it enters, and this pushes another and so on, until a body enters the place left by the first body 'at the very moment the first body leaves it.' Fourth, it implies that the so-called secondary qualities, such as perceived heat, sound, taste, colors and flavors, are not properties of objects at all. They are only confused ideas that exist in the mind due to its interaction with the body. Matter really only has the geometrical properties defined in terms of its essence. Therefore, the secondary qualities are experiential appearances, which must be explained in terms of underlying geometrical primary qualities. For example, Descartes developed a corpuscular theory of heat, which shows that our perceptual idea of heat does not resemble what the heat of body really consists in.

The Real Distinction

Descartes' conception of matter as an inert, dead substance that undergoes mechanically explainable changes makes the contrast between the physical universe and the human mind very sharp. The human mind is conscious, rational and free. Matter is dead, inert, and determined by causal laws. How can we reconcile the two?

Descartes' answer is that the mind must be something essentially non-material. As we have seen, he shows that the essential nature of mental substance is different from that of material substance. In other words, the new conception of matter provides proof of the existence of the soul. Properly understood, the new physics supports religion.

Accordingly, the universe contains at least two kinds of substances: mind, whose essence is to be conscious, and matter, whose essence is spatial. This position is called substance dualism. Thus, according to Descartes, a human being consists of these two distinct substances in intimate causal relations. Changes in the body constantly cause changes in the mind and vice versa.

Descartes gives us three arguments for his substance dualism.

1) The argument from clear and distinct ideas

In the Second Meditation, Descartes argues that his essence is to think. In the Sixth Meditation he takes this conclusion a step further towards proving dualism by arguing that his essence consists solely in thinking. In other words, the one and only attribute without which he cannot continue to exist is that of being conscious. This new argument involves the principle that clear and distinct ideas are true, which was not available to him in the Second Meditation before he had proved the existence of God. This new argument is as follows. We clearly and distinctly perceive that, in thinking of the self as a conscious being, we conceive of it as having all it needs to exist by itself as a substance or complete thing. Because clear and distinct ideas are true, Descartes infers that his essence consists solely in the fact that he is conscious. In other words, he claims to have a clear idea that he, as a conscious being, is really distinct from his body and could exist without it.

2) The argument from doubt

This argument occurs in the *Discourse On the Method*, Part IV, as an application of the method of doubt:

1. I cannot doubt that I (as a mind) exist.
2. I can doubt that my body exists.
3. Therefore, I (as a mind) am distinct from my body.

The argument relies on the principle of the indiscernibility of identicals. This principle states that identicals, such as water and H2O, must have all properties in common. If water had a property that was not shared by H2O then the two could not be identical.

3) The argument from divisibility

The third argument is to be found in the Sixth Meditation. Descartes contends that he is a complete and indivisible thing. Whereas Plato affirmed that the soul has parts, such as perception, emotion, and reason, Descartes denies that these are parts, 'since it is one and the same mind that wills, understands and has sensory perceptions.' To understand this, recall Descartes' image of the wax; the wax stays the same even though it has different shapes. Similarly, according to Descartes, consciousness stays the same, even when what it does alters. However matter, being extended in space, is always divisible. Hence, Descartes concludes that he, as thinking thing, must be different in kind from all matter, including his own body.

1. The mind is an indivisible thing
2. All material objects must be spatially extended
3. Anything that is spatially extended is divisible.
4. Therefore, the mind is not a material object.

Conclusion

By answering the challenge of radical skepticism, Descartes has argued in favor of theses that apparently accomplish his two main philosophical aims. First, through the principle that clear and distinct ideas are true, he can conclude that his physics has a firm epistemological foundation in comparison to Scholasticism. Second, at the same time, he can claim to have shown that the new physics must be compatible with the major claims of religion. God must exist and a proper understanding of matter shows that the soul must be something distinct. In this way, Descartes has apparently fulfilled Bacon's vision.

5

Descartes and Elizabeth: The Nature of Humans

For some time after his death, Descartes was known as a materialist. This may seem strange especially considering that, in the 20th century, his mind-body dualism has become one of the most widely criticized philosophical positions. Indeed, there is some truth to the idea that, in a sense, Descartes was not the simple dualist that he is often painted to be. There are two factors to consider. The first is his views on the nature of animal consciousness. The second is that, in their famous correspondence, his friend Princess Elizabeth of Bohemia convinced him to alter his views. Both issues take us beyond the text of the *Meditations*.

After the death of his daughter in 1640 and the publication of the *Meditations* a year later, Descartes life changed. He was a shy person and he became involved in unwelcome public controversy about the theological implications of his views. During this period, in May 1643, when she was twenty-five, Descartes began his friendship with Princess Elizabeth. He wrote to her frequently, and quite intimately, and may have been in love with her, even though they rarely met. She probably viewed him as her mentor and called him 'the best doctor for my soul.' In 1647, Elizabeth moved away from the Netherlands. As it became clear to Descartes that she would not return to the Netherlands, he began to think of moving back to France himself. He visited Paris in

1648. But the city was in the middle of a revolt and, in 1649, Descartes decided to accept the post as tutor to the young intellectual Queen Christina of Sweden. A year later he died in Sweden.

The Case of Animals

According to Descartes, nature is a complex mechanism and, for this reason, animals, which are a part of nature, may be compared to clockwork. Real birds are like the toy mechanical birds on show in the circus. The difference is one of degree, not one of principle.

Are birds conscious? Are they aware of the environment around them? Surely, they are. In fact, Descartes does not deny that animals have mental states. He actually affirms that they have sense perceptions and that they can imagine and feel. In a letter of November 1646, he writes:

> All the things which dogs, horses and monkeys are taught to perform are only the expression of their fear, their hope or their joy (AT IV 574).

In other words, according to Descartes, animals do have feelings, even though they do not have a non-material mind or soul. Consequently, he thinks that certain mental states can be explained mechanically and are purely material. In this limited sense, he is a materialist. We may conclude, then, that Descartes thinks that some mental states are physical and mechanical, and that others belong to a non-material, non-mechanical mind. This raises an interesting question: Where and how does Descartes draw the line between these two kinds of mental states?

Probably, the best answer is as follows. Animals can have the conscious experience of passions and perceptual ideas. However, because they lack a soul, animals cannot have self-consciousness. An animal can be aware, but it cannot be aware of its awareness, because self-awareness requires the presence of a non-material mind. Notice that this reply commits Descartes to the claim that a mechanical and material theory of consciousness is possible.

How is this line to be drawn? Descartes replies that it should be drawn on the basis of language and understanding. Descartes would admit that it would be possible to construct a mechanical robot behaviorally indistinguishable from any animal. In the case of a human, however, a mechanistic replica would be impossible because:

> It is not conceivable that such a machine should produce different arrangements of words so as to give an appropriately meaningful answer to whatever is said in its presence, as the dullest of men can do. (AT VI 56)

Second, in part V of the *Discourse*, he also says that a machine would reveal that it was not acting through understanding, because inevitably, it would fail to do as well as humans in some tasks, even though in others it might excel. In other words, a computer might do well at playing chess or composing music, but there would be some task that it would be unable to perform, such as making peace between two squabbling individuals. The machine would lack reason which 'is a universal instrument which can be used in all kinds of situations.' According to Descartes, these are the two overt signs by which we can distinguish a being that has a soul from one that does not.

A Substantial Union

Towards the end of his life, under the influence of Princess Elizabeth, Descartes began to think more deeply about the passions, morality and the virtues. As a result he wrote the *Passions of the Soul* (1649). This work and their early correspondence of 1643 focused mostly on the relation between the mind and the body, and in these letters, Descartes reveals a position rather different from the strict mind-body dualism outlined in the previous chapter. Around mid 1645, they started to correspond more frequently, and the new position becomes even more explicit. From that date, Elizabeth became more influential in forming Descartes' views about human nature and the passions. As a result, Descartes became more interested in the effects of the mind upon bodily health, rather than in explaining health in purely physical terms. This is a more fundamental change than it may appear. Previously, Descartes, like Bacon before him, had assumed that the future of human happiness lay with the development of science. Now, his position is that human happiness depends fundamentally on the passions and their control. Whereas the earlier Descartes sought the prolongation of human life through physical medicine, the new Descartes finds wisdom in 'another easier and much surer way, which is not to fear death.' Descartes' later philosophy paves the way to the spiritual philosophy of Spinoza.

In an early letter to Elizabeth, dated 28th June 1643, Descartes refers to three *primitive* notions: the soul, the body, and the union of the two. Descartes refers to a substantial union between the mind and body, as if the two were one primitive substance or object. In other words, rather than talking about a mind *and* a body, we should think of a human being as a body-mind. This is because the embodied mind has very special characteristics. In this case, the whole is more than the sum of the parts. Humans are embodied beings.

In this way, Descartes refines or supplements his official dualist position of the *Meditations*. The official view of Descartes is that the person is a thinking substance or a non-material and non-spatial soul. The new idea is that the human being (as opposed to the person) is a substantial union of mind and body, with special characteristics, had by neither one on its own.

In particular, sensation and imagination occupy this curious half way position. They are neither a purely mental state nor a purely a bodily state. They are characteristic of being embodied. The best examples of this new class of ideas are hunger and thirst. We do not have to perceive that we are hungry and thirsty, in the way that we have to look at the dials of the gas tank of a car. Hunger and thirst are sensations we feel in our body. They arise 'from the union and as it were intermingling of the mind with the body.' We have them because we are embodied. Pure minds would not have them. According to Descartes, perceptual ideas and the passions also fit into this third category of body-mind states. In *The Passions of the Soul*, Descartes emphasizes the essential dependence of many mental functions on the body: imagination, feeling, sensation. Of course, the more he does this, the emptier the disembodied non-material mind seems (and the more boring the after-life seems).

However, once we remember the historical context within which Descartes was writing, his overall strategy makes more sense. The scholastic thinkers of the time confused the mental and the physical, attributing mental properties to matter to explain physical changes. In his natural philosophy, Descartes opposes all such forms of vitalism. Physical changes must be explained mechanically, without any illicit appeal to purposes and mental properties (such as the fear of a vacuum). In other words, Descartes' physics requires a sharp separation of the mental and physical. The same principle applies to physiology and animal behavior. Mental characteristics must only be applied to the mind as such. Only after having separated the mind and the body, could Descartes reunite them.

The Passions

The Passions of the Soul was finished in the winter of 1645. It aims to give a complete account of the mind-body relation along the lines outlined in his correspondence with Elizabeth. Descartes was enthusiastically optimistic about the implications of his new scientific method for psychology. Under Elizabeth's influence, he became interested in the effect of moods and feelings on physical health, wanting to form a theory of psychosomatic medicine. Furthermore, Descartes saw the attitude of the individual towards his or her passions as the key to a happy life. He finishes his work on the passions as follows: 'It is on the passions alone that all the good and harm of this life depends... They dispose us to want those things which nature deems useful to us.'

Descartes' aim is to give an account of the passions that maintains a clear distinction between the mind and the body, that does not make the mistake of dividing the soul into parts, and that recognizes that a human is a body-mind. In Part I of the work, he argues that the passions must be explained in terms of the substantial union of the mind and body, and he provides a general nature of the passions. In Part II, Descartes gives a classification of the passions, and in Part III, an account of specific passions and a discussion of therapeutic questions. Descartes affirms that we have six basic passions, which are wonder, love, hate, desire, joy, and sadness. These six combine to form more complex feelings, such as disdain, pride, and humility. For example, pride is when we love ourselves and desire to remain as we are. Anger is a violent kind of hatred, combined with a desire involving self-love.

The function of the passions is to guide us to want things that are good for us. However, sometimes the passions are an unreliable guide. They lead us to do things that harm us. Descartes does not condemn the passions for this. In fact, he thinks that this is fortunate tendency, as because of it we are forced to develop our capacity to control our emotions. Otherwise, we would merely act always on our passions and never actively employ our will. On the other hand, when the passions are controlled by the rational soul, we can trust them in a way that does not threaten our well-being or our autonomy. These claims will be important for understanding the work of Spinoza.

6

Early Modern French Philosophy

Although Descartes dominates French philosophy of the modern period, there are a host of other very important pre-Enlightenment French thinkers whom we should not neglect. This chapter not only aims to describe the philosophical context of the pre and post-Cartesian periods, but also aims to help us appreciate and chart the enormous influence of France upon the intellectual development of Europe.

In the late 16th century, France was in the midst of religious and political turmoil, called the Wars of Religion. From 1562 to 1598, with the arrival of the Reformation, rival Catholic and Protestant groups of the nobility vied for power. It was in this context that Montaigne wrote his *Essays*.

Montaigne

Between 1580 and 1598, nine editions of Montaigne's *Essays* were published. It was a very popular and influential work, which expressed the spirit of the Renaissance. However, the *Essays* are an intensely personal work because they are, above all, Montaigne writing about himself. It is not an autobiography, but rather a brutally honest and unsystematic description of his bodily functions, feelings, thoughts and character.

As a young child, Michel de Montaigne (1533-92) had a very liberal upbringing and education. He was allowed to explore freely the world of knowledge. As a young man, he studied law at university and hated it. Nevertheless, he entered politics. However, after the death of his father in 1568, Montaigne retired from public life and the religious strife that divided France. In the library of the castle that he had inherited, he studied Erasmus, Plutarch, Seneca, Lucretius, and many of the classic pagan writers of ancient Greece and Rome. After 1570, he started to write essays on what happened to interest him.

As part of his *Essays*, Montaigne takes his reader on a tour of ancient philosophy, at first not able to settle on any definite views for himself. Initially, he finds wisdom in the ethics of Stoicism but, as the *Essays* proceed, he is drawn increasingly towards skepticism. He claims that all knowledge is based on the senses and notes their unreliability. He observes that the instincts are often a surer guide in life than reason. Noting the great variety of philosophical, moral, and scientific views, he concludes that 'the greatest part of what we know is the least part of what we do not know.' Finally, like the ancient Greek skeptic Pyrrho, he decides to suspend judgment and simply to observe. Paradoxically, in this spirit of skepticism, he resolves to observe the religion of his own time and place, Catholicism. It was not a question of faith, but rather, geography.

Montaigne's *Essays* present skepticism with a very human and reasonable face. In this way, they oppose any religious dogmatism and articulate the humanism of the Renaissance. The very clarity of his writing and the freedom of his thought both express and pave the way to the values of the Enlightenment. These qualities of his work had a more subversive and liberating effect on French and European thinking than any revolutionary political tract or philosophical treatise might have had.

Montaigne wrote his *Essays* in 1580, thirty years before Kepler and Galileo published their astronomical findings and sixty years before Descartes' *Meditations*. The scientific revolution was only an uncertain seed, while the Church was just beginning to grasp the serious implications of the Copernican Revolution. The Renaissance was still spreading northwards from Italy, and Europe was struggling with the Reformation.

Descartes, Mersenne and Gassendi

France's Religious Wars drew towards a close in 1593, when Henry of Navare (1553-1610) became King Henry IV of France, after a siege of Paris. Raised as a Protestant Huguenot, Henry converted to Catholicism, the dominant religion of the country, in order to gain control of the throne. An uneasy peace finally came in 1598, when Henry issued the Edict of Nantes, which authorized the Protestant faith and awarded the Huguenots full control of certain towns.

After Henry was assassinated, the young and weak Louis XIII came to the French throne. In 1624, Cardinal Richelieu became Louis' strong Prime Minister, and he began intelligently to impose order, Catholicism and centralized power on a weakened country. Under his control, France became a major European power.

Given this context, we can perhaps understand Descartes' decision of 1628 to leave his native France and settle in the more liberal and quiet atmosphere of the Netherlands. Nevertheless, Descartes left behind an intellectual community of natural philosophers or scientists, which included his friends Mersenne and Gassendi.

Pierre Gassendi (1592-1655) was the son of a peasant in the South of France. However, at the age of 16, he was appointed a university lecturer and, by the time he was 25, he was Professor of Philosophy at the University of Aix en Provence. In 1645, he was appointed Chair of Mathematics in Paris. However, due to illness, he returned south, where he wrote his major philosophical works.

He drew philosophical inspiration from the atomism of Lucretius and the ethics of Epicurus. At the same time, he was a priest and a humble and devout follower of the Church. He claimed that there were two truths: those of reason and those of faith. From 1647-9 he wrote three major works on the atomism of Lucretius. Gassendi's emphasis on experimental science and atomism, and his rejection of the Aristotelian Scholasticism made him the most influential French thinker of the modern period after Descartes.

Pascal and Port-Royal

When, in 1643, Louis XIV came to the throne at the age of five, France was the dominant nation of Europe. Germany was part of the Austro-Hungarian Roman Empire, which consisted of over 400 fragmented states, and which was recovering from the Thirty Years War. England was at the beginning of its Civil War. After the earlier firm guidance of Richelieu (1585-1642) during the reign of Louis XIII, France was already close to having national unity, and this was at only the beginning of Louis XIV's long reign, which ended in 1715. So, France was about to enjoy a period of great stability during which science and the arts flourished, but within the context of an absolute monarchy.

As a young Catholic king, Louis XIV was determined to maintain national unity and suppress the Protestant religion in France. However, his wish met the resistance of the Port Royal and the philosopher Pascal.

Port Royal

Port Royal was a little known Catholic convent about 16 miles from Paris, which had been founded in 1204. The convent had been on the decline for some time. In 1608, the new young abbess, Jacqueline Arnauld had a powerful religious experience, and she revived the nunnery and imposed strict discipline. In her newly found religious zeal, she enlisted the support of her large and powerful family to spread reforms to other convents. Her brother, Antoine Arnauld II, became the vocal philosopher and theologian of Port Royal. The convent opened a branch in Paris, attracted male disciples, and Arnauld wrote an influential logic text, *The Art of Thinking*. In 1638, the Port Royal community began to open schools in the region, which were considered the best in the country.

The growing Port Royal community was influenced in its beliefs by a form of mystical Catholic puritanism, called Jansenism. The Jansenists followed the doctrine of predetermination based on the teachings of St Paul and St. Augustine. According to this doctrine, at the time of Creation, God had predetermined which souls were to be saved and which were to be damned. In contrast, the mainstream Catholic Church taught the doctrine of free will, according to which the individual had the moral responsibility to avoid sin and earn salvation through meritorious good works.

The eloquent and vociferous Arnauld entered into a public conflict with the Jesuits. He accused them of moral leniency and theological inconsistency, and he attacked the moral standards of the royal court. For their part, the Jesuits, like the King, regarded Jansenism as a form of Protestant Calvinism thinly disguised as a Catholic sect. In 1653, the Pope declared as heresy certain propositions from St Augustine. The ensuing dispute divided France and absorbed the powerful intellect of Pascal.

Pascal

From a very early age Blaise Pascal (1623-62) was intensely interested in science, His father was a student of geometry and physics, and the young child listened to his father's conversations with Gassendi, Mersenne and Descartes, At the age of 15, he wrote a treatise on conic sections. When he was 19, Pascal invented a calculating machine, which used cogs and wheels. In 1648, he developed the mathematics of probability, also independently discovered by Fermat.

Pascal continued his work in mathematics and experimental science until around 1654, when he was nearly killed in a carriage accident. Thereafter, his passions turned to religion, nourished by the reoccurrence of an illness that left him in severe pain for much of the time.

In 1654, he became a member of the Port Royal community. His sister became a Port Royal nun. In 1656, at the urging of Arnauld, he composed his *Provincial Letters*, defending Jansenism, and attacking the Jesuits for moral and theological laxity. Partly because of their eloquence and passion, Pascal's letters had an immense influence on French public opinion, contributing to the decline of the Jesuits in France.

In 1656, Pascal began to write his famous *Pensées,* a defense of religious belief. In this work, Pascal attacks science, claiming that it is based on reason, which in turn is based on the notoriously fallible senses. The world is full of mysteries that are unintelligible to reason. It cannot comprehend the relation between mind and body, the nature of morality and God, nor the meaning of human life. Instead of reason, we should rely on religious feeling. Pascal writes 'the heart has its reasons, which reason does not know.'

In the *Pensées*, Pascal challenges nonbelievers to his famous wager. Faith and religious belief cannot be proved. However, belief in God is a wise bet. Pascal weighs the gain and loss in betting on the existence of God. If God exists, the reward for faith is eternal salvation and the cost of unbelief is eternal damnation. On the other hand, if God does not exist, the believer has lost little and the nonbeliever has gained almost nothing. Pascal concludes 'wager, then, without hesitation that He exists.' He advises nonbelievers who find it difficult to believe nevertheless to observe the customs of the Church, for belief will follow.

We can regard Jansenism as a final attempt of the Reformation to make headway in Catholic France. As King Louis grew older he became more intolerant and, in 1709, he disbanded the Port Royal. Pascal's passionate critique of reason went more or less unheard until Rousseau (see Chapter 19). His engaged and biting style of writing influenced generations of French writers. Even the notorious critic of religion, Voltaire, called Pascal's *Letters* 'the best written book that has yet appeared in France.'

Malebranche

Around 1650, Descartes' philosophy was very popular in France because of its reconciliation of science and religion and its rationalistic vision of the unity of the sciences. However, Pascal denounced Descartes for trying to dispense with God. Pascal argued that, once Descartes' mechanical universe was put into motion, it has no further need of God. From 1670, religious writers increasingly condemned Descartes' work. On the other hand, Cartesian philosophy remained popular amongst the more secular and less orthodox thinkers.

This conflict forms the background for the thought of Nicholas Malebranche (1638-1715). He was raised a staunch Catholic. When he read Descartes, he also became a Cartesian. Descartes' rationalism inspired Malebranche to defend his Catholic faith rationally. After ten years' work, he published *The Search for Truth* (1674), a book of four volumes.

According to Malebranche, Descartes' dualist philosophy had one major flaw. It could not explain how the non-material mind causally interacts with the physical body. Malebranche was convinced that the mind and body were distinct substances, as Descartes had argued. However, Malebranche was also convinced that they could not interact. Thus, he advanced the theory, called occasionalism, that there was no such interaction. He argued that God created the mental and physical worlds as two independent and parallel, but perfectly synchronized, series of events.

Earlier, the Flemish philosopher Geulincx had claimed that these two realms, the mental and the physical, were like two divinely synchronized clocks that function completely independently of each other, but keep the same time. As we shall see, Geulincx's idea had an important influence on Spinoza and Leibniz, as well as Malebranche.

However, Malebranche also argued against the mechanistic determinism inherent in Geulincx's analysis and analogy. Instead, Malebranche claimed that God must be the direct cause of both mental states and physical events. In other words, God must constantly maintain the two parallel and independent streams of existence, the mental and physical, in a perfect synchronicity. Given that the mind and body are distinct but causally independent, and given that mechanistic determinism is false, Malebranche argued that there was no other plausible alternative to his theory. Thus, he concluded that the Divine power is constantly acting in the universe through physical and mental processes. This means that motion is the physical expression of God's power and that our thoughts are manifestations of God's power in us. In this sense, God is the only true agent in the universe.

Malebranche's unorthodox religious views attracted much criticism from both the traditional Catholics in France and from Arnauld, the defender of Port Royal. Malebranche became a celebrity. Despite the criticisms of his position, Malebranche's philosophy gained adherents, and towards the end of his life, he had long discussions with the young Irish philosopher, Berkeley (see Chapter 15).

Despite its influence on later philosophers, such as Leibniz and Berkeley, in general terms Malebranche's religious philosophy was out of tune with the mechanistic and scientific spirit of the time. Perhaps, more than anything, it signaled and emphasized that there were serious problems with Descartes' dualism.

Bayle

In contrast, Pierre Bayle (1647-1706) was ahead of his time. His pioneering work laid some of the foundations for the later French Enlightenment (see Chapter 19). Bayle was a Protestant Huguenot, who lost his faith after reading Descartes. In 1682, after moving to Holland, he published his first major work in which he argued that religious belief was not necessary for the preservation of moral standards; an atheistic society would have similar moral to a Christian one. In 1684, Bayle launched, edited and wrote one of the major journals of the time, *News from the Republic of Letters*, which was published in Holland. For three years, the *News* informed its readers of important developments in science, philosophy, history and literature.

After 1693, Bayle shut himself in his room, writing day in and out what was to become his most famous and influential work, the massive *The Historical and Critical Dictionary*, published in 1697. It is a wide-ranging, witty and unsystematic review of ideas, thinkers, mythology, religion and literature. It is also thoroughly heretical. He throws doubt on the Biblical miracle stories, the Trinity, the Fall of Adam, the omnipotence of God and much more besides. However, he expresses his skepticism indirectly by quoting and describing the views of others. Bayle's *Dictionary* had a deep influence on European thought. More than anything, it inspired a generation of French Enlightenment thinkers.

7

Hobbes: Politics as Science

Thomas Hobbes (1588-1679) had a very long life. As a young man, around 1618-20, he worked as a secretary for Francis Bacon. In the 1630's, he visited Paris, where he met Gassendi, and Descartes' friend Mersenne. He also met Galileo in Italy and, in 1641, he wrote one of the set of Objections to Descartes' *Meditations*. Towards the end of his life, Hobbes became embroiled in a controversy with the chemist Boyle, who was a friend of Locke. In 1666, the year that Newton made many of his important scientific discoveries, Hobbes was accused of atheism and, thus, of being responsible for the Fire of London and the Plague. Hobbes was born during the reign of Queen Elizabeth and when he died, James II was king. Hobbes lived during the reigns of five monarchs, as well as the period when England was a republic. During his life-time, England underwent a civil war, which resulted in a republic and the execution of Charles I (1649) and saw the restoration of the monarch Charles II eleven years later. In France, in 1646, Hobbes worked as tutor for the exiled future Charles II.

These events show us that Hobbes lived during the time of both scientific and political revolution. Like Locke after him, Hobbes participated as a philosopher in both of these revolutions. As a result, he had a clear major philosophical aim: to show how the principles of modern science can be applied to politics. He regarded political theory as potentially the most useful of all the sciences because it can bring peace, but only if it is based on scientific principles.

To achieve this aim, Hobbes had an ambitious and controversial strategy. He divided philosophy into three parts: physics, psychology and politics and argued that the principles of physics were necessary for a proper understanding of human psychology, which turn was necessary for political theory.

The Nature of Science

Hobbes tried to overthrow the scholastic conception of the world and the dogmatic epistemological attitudes it fermented by developing a view of science that opposes the views of both Bacon and Descartes. At the same time, Hobbes' philosophy is important because it is both thoroughly materialistic and mechanistic.

1) Empiricist Rationalism

Unlike Bacon, Hobbes thinks that natural science should not just collect empirical data, but instead it should be concerned with demonstrating scientific knowledge from principles and definitions. Hobbes claims that scientific knowledge is gained through reasoning, which is computational and consists of addition and subtraction. For example, the concept of a human being is formed by adding the concepts of rational, animate and body. In this respect, his philosophy of science is rationalist. This point had an important influence on Leibniz.

At the same time, unlike Descartes, Hobbes has an empiricist theory of scientific concepts. Scientific knowledge needs the appropriate kind of evidence, as well as the relevant concepts, which are derived from sense experience. Hobbes thinks that all we know of nature depends on sense perception, and this includes the knowledge of principles. In this respect, all knowledge is based on sense experience, without which there could be no science. Nevertheless, perception alone does not amount to scientific knowledge. Because science aims to explain natural phenomena, it should seek the causes of events and, for this reason, mere observational knowledge of facts does not constitute science.

2) Mechanism

According to Hobbes, the universe consists only of matter in motion, and causal influence can be transmitted from one body to another only through motion. For example, heat is transmitted by the movement of particles. All causation is mechanistic. For example, there must be small particles, or some medium, which transmits the influence from one body to another. Thus, there can be no genuine action at a distance. This mechanistic theory of causation is in complete contrast to the scholastic view according to which things move in nature because of their natural ends or purposes. Hobbes says that purposes are only applicable to animate beings that have a will. Even more radically, Hobbes argues that, even in the case of animate beings, such final causes or purposes are really efficient causes. In other words, Hobbes believes that his mechanistic view should be applied to humans.

A cause consists in the motions that are necessary and sufficient for a specific effect. Thus, causes determine their effects. Hobbes was a causal determinist. Events appear contingent because we are ignorant of their causes. However, Hobbes distinguishes necessary and contingent propositions. A necessary proposition is one in which the subject contains the predicate. For example, 'a human is a living creature' is a necessarily true proposition. On the other hand, a contingent true proposition may become false, because the predicate is not part of the meaning or definition of the subject.

According to Hobbes, scientific knowledge is concerned only with necessary propositions. Scientific definitions should include the cause of things. Hobbes thinks that science consists of only necessary propositions because all scientific claims follow from definitions. From universal definitions, we can deduce hypothetical claims about particular things, which have the form 'If X has property F then it will have property G.' Hence, scientific knowledge is universal and hypothetical. This view of science excludes all empirical propositions and may strike us as strange, because observation apparently plays an insignificant role in this theory. However, Hobbes distinguishes two kinds of knowledge: knowledge of fact and of principles. Knowledge of contingent propositions or facts, for example, in history, would not qualify as science. Science is restricted to knowledge of universal principles and their consequences. Hobbes' view of science was influenced by the pioneering work of Galileo, who searched for fundamental mathematical patterns underlying observable phenomena. Additionally, Hobbes' view of science is based on Euclid's geometry. He argues that the idea of motion is inherent in the science of geometry because lines consist of the motion of points, and plane surfaces consist of the motion of lines.

3) Materialism

Hobbes claims that everything in the world consists of material bodies in motion. Physics is the science that states the laws that govern such motion. The only way one thing can cause a change in another is through movement. Hobbes affirms that a substance is corporeal or material if and only if it has spatial magnitude or extension.

Hobbes argues for his materialistic claim that everything that exists is physical on the basis of his mechanistic view of causation. Anything non-physical would not be able to have causal relations with anything physical, because it could not participate in any physical causal mechanism. In this way, Hobbes claims that materialism is the logical consequence of the new science, and he opposes Descartes' mind/body dualism.

In the historical context, Hobbes' materialist thesis is a very bold one. He tries to answer three objections to his materialism.

1. The first is that materialism is incompatible with the existence of space and time. The statement that everything is made of matter seems to contradict the claim that space exists, because space itself is not made of matter. In reply, Hobbes denies that space is real. Space is the appearance of externality. Things in our imagination appear to be in space and, therefore, space is not part of the real world. Hobbes does not mean that physical objects are unreal, nor that physical objects do not have spatial magnitude. Rather his claim is that our concept of space is only an abstraction from our perceptual experience of real bodies with real extension or magnitude.

2. The second objection is that materialism cannot be made compatible with the fact that we have sensations and conscious experience. In reply, Hobbes argues that his view of causation implies that sensation must be a physical motion. Given that sensations are caused, they must be an instance of matter in motion in the brain. He says that experience and ideas are motions of some material substance in the head (E.W. IV, 2). Hobbes' theory of perception is fundamentally realist. He assumes that physical objects exist independently of our perception of them. He does not try to explain objects in terms of our perceptions or ideas, but rather he tries to explain ideas in terms of the movement of material bodies. For example, memory occurs when our organs retain some of the movement occasioned by the external object. Concentration occurs when the registration of other external objects on the sense organs is made impossible because the movement in the nerves caused by the first object is so strong. Imagination is nothing but decaying sense (EW III,4). The capacity to imagine something new such as a centaur, a horse's body with a man's head, Hobbes explains as similar to two currents converging to produce a third flow that is a combination of the two.

3. The third objection is that materialism precludes the possibility of God. In the *Leviathan*, Hobbes tries to explain religion in terms that are compatible with his mechanistic philosophy. First, he gives a naturalistic explanation of religious beliefs; our idea of an invisible agent is a result of our wish to find explanations for all natural events. Second, God is a material being. In support of this view, Hobbes claims that the idea of an incorporeal substance is contradictory. A substance is a body and must occupy space and be subject to change. This definition of the word 'body,' however, allows for the possibility of intangible and invisible material bodies, which Hobbes calls 'spirits.' Third, at *Leviathan* 12.6, Hobbes argues that God is the cause of the world and that God's commands are the laws of nature, which are known through reason. Fourth, Hobbes excludes the study of God from science and philosophy, which are concerned with the generation of things. Theology cannot yield scientific knowledge because the idea of God is the conception of something without external cause. Furthermore, there is no idea of the infinite and, because of this, reason can only inform us of what God cannot be. At *Leviathan* 12.7, Hobbes claims God should be worshipped and honored rather than investigated. Hobbes affirms that religious language has a laudatory role. It is employed to praise God rather than to describe Him.

Psychology and Motivation

Hobbes' psychological theory has two parts: sensation and motivation. We have already examined briefly his view of sensation. His theory of motivation forms the bridge from his physical mechanics to his political philosophy, and it consists of three steps.

The first step is from physics to psychology. Hobbes' physics includes the idea of instantaneous movement, that is motion through a point in space, which lasts an instant of time. Hobbes calls this 'endeavor.' He claims that our movements towards and away from the objects of desire and aversion are caused by such endeavors in the body. The second step introduces the ideas of pleasure and pain. Pleasure and pain are movements of the blood around the heart caused by endeavors towards or away from things known by experience to be pleasurable or painful. These motions generate desire and aversion. In Chapter 6 of the *Leviathan*, Hobbes introduces the third step. He defines six basic passions in terms of different types of desire and aversion and pleasure and pain. Appetite and aversion presuppose the absence of their objects. Love and hate presuppose the presence of their objects. Joy and grief are the feelings of pleasure and pain based on the expectation of an end, and on the awareness of the personal power to produce that end. On this basis, Hobbes tries to explain other features of human psychological life

In Chapter 14 of the *Leviathan*, Hobbes seems to argue that every person acts for his or her personal good. He may mean that every person acts solely out of a desire for personal power or a fear of harm. Alternatively, he may mean that humans have a primary goal of being first in life's race for resources and power.

The Science of Politics

This egoism implies the inevitability of natural conflict or war, given that goods are scarce and that no one person has sufficient natural advantage to be able dominate all other people (*Leviathan*, Chapter 13). Naturally and rationally, people are in a state of war with one another. Our natural plight is 'solitary, poor, nasty, brutish and short' and, to avoid it, people agree to make a covenant and be governed by a sovereign in a commonwealth (Leviathan 13.9).

The essence of Hobbes' political theory is that we form a government through a covenant, which is a contract according to which individuals transfer certain natural rights to a sovereign in exchange for a gain, which is peace and security. We transfer to a sovereign all our natural rights. Furthermore, reason dictates and God commands us to seek peace, and this requires us to give up all our natural rights to a sovereign in a covenant and to keep to that covenant, so long as others do so. In short, the inevitability of war explains why we should enter into a covenant in the first place; the idea of the moral laws of nature explain why should keep to that covenant; and the concept of natural rights explains the nature of the covenant.

The covenant results in a government that is absolute. A sovereign cannot give up his or her right to self-governance, because otherwise, he or she would not be the sovereign. Hobbes' theory hinges on the idea that the only alternative to this absolute conception of governmental power is something even worse: the natural state of war. Although the sovereign does have an obligation to obey the laws of nature and ought to do his best to protect his subjects, nevertheless the sovereign must be above the civil law. This is because the sovereign is not part of society's covenant. The covenant is an agreement between the people to transfer to a sovereign their natural rights to enforce morality.

8

Spinoza: Against Dualism

Baruch de Spinoza (1632–1677) was a saintly person, who lived a simple and quiet life and who developed a very unorthodox religious vision. Spinoza rejects the essence of Bacon's utopia that human progress consists in enjoying the material benefits of the new science. According to Spinoza, such scientific progress is worthless if the result is merely that human beings acquire power over nature without improving their character and their relation to their own passions. For Spinoza, liberation consists in freedom from the bondage of desire and in union with the whole of Nature.

In this way, Spinoza's main aim is to develop a non-authoritarian ethic. However, he thinks that a correct understanding of the ethical life depends on metaphysics, which is non-dualist in nature. At the same time, this metaphysics will reveal the relation between religion and science. It will show how science and religion do not conflict.

Spinoza's Life

Spinoza was born in the Jewish community of Amsterdam in 1632. His early education was almost entirely religious, but his later teachers included Manasseh ben Israel, a major figure in 17th century Judaism, who was also well connected in the secular world. He may have introduced Spinoza to mathematics, physics, and non-Jewish philosophy.

In 1654, his father died. Spinoza's sister claimed the whole inheritance and Spinoza took her to court. When he won the case, he gave his sister the whole legacy, except for one bed. To earn his living, Spinoza chose the trade of making and polishing lenses for spectacles, microscopes, and telescopes. During this period, Spinoza studied Bacon, Descartes and Hobbes. He begun to doubt his religion and, in 1656, he was excommunicated from the synagogue and Jewish community, and his family disowned him. He began to write philosophy with the aim of discovering the 'truly good.' During this period, he reached the conclusion that the highest good was union with the whole of Nature.

In 1670, Spinoza published anonymously *A Treatise on Theology and Politics*. It undertakes to reveal the human fallibility of the Bible without 'prejudice to piety and the public peace.' With a careful and detailed analysis of the text, he questions the orthodox view that the early books of the Old Testament were written by Moses and points out many contradictions and historical impossibilities in both the Old and New Testaments. He challenges the miracle stories, claiming that all events happen according to natural law. He concludes that the essence of religion consists in living virtuously and not in any doctrine. Needless to say, this heretical text and declaration of the freedom of thought was banned and attracted severe criticism from Protestants, Catholics, as well as the Jewish community.

Spinoza was apparently working on the *Ethics* intermittently from 1662 to 1675. He attempted to publish it in 1675, but local theologians thwarted this plan. In 1677, Spinoza died of consumption, probably complicated by chronic inhalation of glass dust. The *Ethics* and the *Tractatus Politicus* were published the following year.

As we shall see, Spinoza's metaphysics had a direct influence on Leibniz. His Biblical criticism inspired French Enlightenment thinkers. However, the power of his philosophy was not appreciated until the time of Goethe and Hegel and, in England, until that of the Romantic poets, such as Wordsworth (see Chapter 22).

Against Cosmic Dualism

The basic claim of the *Ethics* is that human perfection consists in union with God or Nature as a whole. This union can be achieved only by the individual liberating him or herself from the influences of the passions and desires. Spinoza tries to demonstrate these claims by establishing a metaphysics, which yields a new conception of human nature, which forms the basis of his view of the passions and his ethical theory. Therefore, we shall start by examining Spinoza's metaphysics.

Spinoza's metaphysics is monist, in stark contrast to Descartes' dualism. Descartes' thought contains two dualisms: mind/body and God/World, which are similar to each other. Spinoza eliminates both of these dualisms, but he begins with the second. In the first part of the *Ethics* he argues for two basic propositions: that there can be only one substance and that this substance is God. Consequently, Spinoza's main argument in part I of the *Ethics* consists in two stages. In the first, he tries to prove that there can only be one substance and, in the second, that this one substance has features that allow us to identify it with God.

A) There is only One Substance

Before we examine his argument, we need to understand Spinoza's philosophical vocabulary. He defines 'substance' as that which exists independently and is conceived through itself. Attributes are the essential properties of a substance, and a mode is the modification of an attribute; for example, if blue were an attribute, light and dark blue would be modifications of that attribute. They are different specifications of the attribute. Given these definitions, Spinoza argues that there is only one substance. For the sake of clarity, his proof can be divided into two steps.

i) The first argument: first step

1. If there were two substances then they could not causally interact with each other (proposition I, 6).
2. Everything must have a cause.
3. Therefore, substance must be its own cause and at least one substance must exist (proposition I, 7).

The most contentious premise in this argument is the first. Spinoza attempts to prove it by demonstrating that there cannot be two substances with the same attribute (proposition I, 5), This is a pivotal point because proposition I, 5 is also a premise in the second step, given below. He argues for it by claiming that nothing can distinguish two substances with the same attribute. Two substances with the same attribute cannot be distinguished by their attribute. Nor can they be distinguished by their modes because modes are nothing but modifications of an attribute. There cannot be two substances with the same attribute.

Given this, Spinoza argues for premise 1 above by claiming that two substances can only causally interact with each other if they share an attribute. The point is that, to interact causally, they must have something in common. This insight is crucial to Spinoza's rejection of

Descartes' mind/body dualism, because, according to Descartes, the mind and the body have entirely different essences (to be conscious and to be extended) and yet they interact causally. Spinoza's historically influential criticism of this position is that, if they have nothing in common, then the mind and body cannot have causal effects on each other.

Now Spinoza's reasoning for premise 1 should be clear. Two substances can only interact if they have the same attribute, but there cannot be two substances with the same attribute (I,5). Consequently, if there were two substances then they could not causally interact with each other, and premise 1 is apparently established. Given that it is, and given that everything must have a cause, substance must be its own cause. Now we can turn to the second step to demonstrate that there is only one substance.

ii) The first argument: second step

1. Substance must be its own cause (the conclusion of the first step).
2. If substance is its own cause, then it must have infinite attributes (proposition I, 8).
3. Two substances with the same attributes could not be distinguished (proposition I, 5).
4. Therefore, there can only be one substance (proposition I, 11)

The crucial premise in this step is the fourth. Spinoza argues that if substance were finite, then it would have to be limited by another self-causing substance of the same kind, which is impossible. Furthermore, Spinoza argues that anything that consists of several individuals must have an external cause. The cause of a plurality must be external. Therefore, there can only be one thing that is its own cause.

B) The One Substance is God

Next, Spinoza argues that the nature of this one substance is such that we can identify it as God. This is basically because it satisfies all the requirements for being God. What is God? First, God is a being that exists necessarily. Second, God must be infinite in such a way that no greater being can be imagined. Third, God is such that there is necessarily only one of Him. On this basis, we can reconstruct Spinoza's argument as follows:

1. The three criteria mentioned above are necessary and sufficient conditions for something's being God.
2. The one substance satisfies the three criteria and nothing else can.
3. Therefore, the one substance is God.

Spinoza's text does not explicitly contain the above argument because he does not separate steps A and B above, as we have done for the sake of clarity. Nevertheless, the above argument represents his reasoning.

It is worth stepping back to consider briefly how Spinoza has reached his conclusions. Spinoza has seen that Descartes dualist positions are incompatible with a combination of two basic factors: the definition of substance as something independent, and the rationalist view of causation. According to this conception, causes determine their effects in much the same way that a set of premises entails a conclusion. In other words, causation is like logical entailment. Given this view of causation and the definition of substance, we can appreciate the strength of Spinoza's position. In a sense, a cause already contains its effects. Therefore, because a substance is independent, it can never be the effect of something else. If there existed more than one substance, then they could not be in causal interaction with each other. This point is important for understanding the thought of Leibniz.

Implications

If there is only one substance, what are material objects and individual minds? Objects and minds cannot be parts of the one infinite substance because it must be indivisible, without any parts. If the one substance were divisible, its parts would be also substances. Therefore, substance must be indivisible (*Ethics* I.13). This conclusion had an important influence on Leibniz. So, if minds and bodies are not substances, nor part of the one substance, what are they? Spinoza claims that they are only finite modes. They are finite modifications of the attributes of God. In effect, this means that they are only like properties of the one substance. In this sense, Spinoza implies that finite modes are not real. The world really is a single individual that exists necessarily and timelessly and is indivisible and infinite. This suggests that the viewpoint of 'the common order of nature,' or our normal view of the world as consisting of finite and transitory things, is an illusion. Hence, Spinoza seems to imply that particular things are not really objects at all. They are properties of God, expressed in determinate ways. This book is a modification of an attribute of the one substance. It is the attribute extension modified in a determinate way. It is adjectival.

Against Mind/Body Dualism

Now we can turn to Part II of the *Ethics* concerning human nature. Effectively, Spinoza has already argued against Descartes' mind/body substance dualism, Spinoza has tried to prove that two substances with different attributes cannot causally interact and, furthermore, that there is only substance, God. Given these points, Descartes' dualism must be false. However, this does not show us how we should conceive of the relation between minds and bodies, given the falsity of Cartesian substance dualism.

To explain Spinoza's positive view about the mind and body, we must recall that he argues that God must have infinite attributes. Because God is infinite, there are infinite ways of conceiving Him. However, we are acquainted with only two of His attributes, thought and extension. Given this, Spinoza argues that the mind and the body are the same finite mode viewed under the two different attributes, mind and extension. In effect, he concludes that a dual aspect theory of mind must be true. To understand this, we need to consider the nature of extension and that of thought.

Extension and the Unity of Science

Spinoza says that God is the immanent and not the transcendental cause of all things (*Ethics* I.18). However, he also says that every individual finite mode must be conditioned by another finite mode ad infinitum (*Ethics* I.28). By this he means that any finite mode must be caused by an earlier state of the universe. So where does God as immanent cause fit into this picture? God is not the external cause of any physical change, but rather the Divine Nature, under the attribute of spatial extension, is the basic laws of physics. A particular event determines another only given these general laws of Nature. In other words, antecedent conditions plus causal laws jointly entail a particular fact. In Spinoza's terminology, particular finite modes and the Divine Nature, specifically the nature of the attribute extension, together determine the existence of any finite mode. In this sense, rather than being the creator of the world, God is its immanent cause.

In this way, Spinoza is committed to the idea of a complete and unified physical science. Spinoza thinks that any physical change is a completely determined effect within a closed set of physical causes and laws, and this implies the possibility of a complete and scientific physical explanation. Contrast this claim with Descartes, who thinks that the physical world is subject continually to influences from without, i.e. from non-material minds and God.

Furthermore, Spinoza claims that each attribute must be conceived through itself (*Ethics* I.10). He means that, for instance, when some physical event is to be explained, this must be done through the attribute of extension and its modes alone. The physical explanation should not involve a reference to the mental.

The Nature of the Mind

At *Ethics* II.7, Spinoza says that the order and connection of ideas is the same as the order and connection of extended things. Thought and extension are not two separate substances, but one substance comprehended through different attributes. More specifically, an extended mode and the idea of that mode are one and the same expressed through different attributes. There is only one chain of modes, but it can be viewed in different ways.

The human mind and body are simply a special case of the one order in Nature being viewed through different attributes. The mind is the same mode as the body comprehended through the attribute of thought rather than that of physical extension.

Thus, Spinoza rejects Descartes' substance dualism, but he asserts an attribute dualism, according to which thought and extension are two attributes of the one substance. Particular minds and bodies are not distinct substances, but the same mode conceived through the two attributes, thought and extension. He also rejects Descartes' claim that the mind and body interact. Since the mind and the body are the same mode, there can be no question of any interaction between them and, furthermore, each attribute must be conceived through itself.

According to Spinoza, we can view a human being through the attribute of extension as a material body, subject to and governed entirely by physical laws. Alternatively, we can conceive of a person through the attribute of thought as an idea, governed entirely by the laws of thought. These two ways of conceiving the same finite mode are self-contained and, thus, there can be no interaction between the physical and the mental.

The same point applies to the universe as a whole. Under the attribute of extension, the universe is a closed physical system. But under the attribute of thought, it is one complex idea. Neither, of course, is God because He has infinite attributes. Rather, they are like two faces or aspects of God.

Mind and Body

Spinoza's general theory of mind has some strange implications. One consequence of his theory is that every extended mode must also be capable of being apprehended under the attribute of thought, as an idea. For every extended mode, there must be an idea, with which it is identical. For example, an idea (for instance, of a circle) and its object (the circle itself) are one and the same thing regarded under different attributes. For this reason, Spinoza claims that all things are to different degrees animated (*Ethics* II.13). This point also had an important influence on Leibniz, and should be contrasted with Hobbes' claim that the universe consists of solely inert matter.

As a consequence of the above, the mind and the body are the same individual, but the object of the mind is always the body itself. The mind is a complex idea, and the object of that idea is simply the body. For example, in the case of perception we are aware of our own body as it is affected by something else. For instance, when perceiving a tree, the object of my mind is not the tree itself, but rather is my own body, as affected by the tree.

Spinoza's general theory of the mind has another strange implication. In asserting the existence of only one substance, Spinoza denies that human minds are substances. Minds are modes of thought. According to Spinoza, the human mind does not *have* ideas; instead, it *is* an idea, albeit a complex one. We should assert that human minds are thoughts. Consequently, ideas exist, but they are not owned or had by finite minds. Spinoza has a non-ownership theory of the mind.

Determinism

Finally, Spinoza's metaphysics is deterministic. Everything must have a sufficient reason. At *Ethics* I.33, he says that things could not occur in any other way. Nothing in the universe is contingent. Apparently, he means that this world is the only possible world. All apparent contingency is the consequence of our ignorance of the order of causes. In this, Spinoza opposes the Cartesian notion of free will. All human behavior is part of the chain of natural causes, and as such it is determined. We only think we are free because we are not conscious of the causes of our actions. Spinoza likens our situation to that of a stone in flight: the stone wishes to be in motion and falsely believes that its free desire is the continuing cause of its motion. The mental and the extended do not form two distinct realms that can interact. For this reason, Spinoza says that the will is not a free cause.

From Epistemology to Ethics

Spinoza's ethics is a union of his theories of metaphysics, knowledge, and emotions. His main ethical thesis is that, by having adequate knowledge of our negative emotions, we can become freer and thereby achieve union with God or Nature.

Theory of Knowledge

Spinoza's theory of knowledge is an important link between his metaphysics and his ethics. From the side of his metaphysics, this is because the order of ideas and the order of extended modes are one and the same. Therefore, knowledge must consist of clear and adequate ideas that reflect the order of nature. From the side of his ethics, Spinoza claims that, by having more clear and adequate ideas of Nature, we may attain greater freedom. With these two criteria in mind, Spinoza sets out a threefold classification of knowledge, in note 2 of *Ethics* II.40.

1. Imagination
Imagination includes knowledge from sense perception, which is an inadequate form of knowledge (II.19 and II.24–28). Sense perception is 'consequence without premises.' It gives us no knowledge of causes and, thus, is radically incomplete. Furthermore, the ideas of perception arise only because of the impact of external things on the body. Hence, they are confused because they reflect no rational order. Nevertheless they inform us of the existence of particular finite modes.

2. Reason
Reason consists of universal, timeless, necessary truths that follow from each other in a deductive system, as in mathematics and the physical sciences. This kind of knowledge is clear and distinct and follows a proper logical order, rather than obeying the laws of psychological association. It is internally rather than externally determined. The ideas of reason are adequate because they have coherence, clarity, and distinctness.

3. Intuition
In Part V, Spinoza discusses intuitive knowledge. Such knowledge has much in common with reason: it is eternal, necessarily true, and internally determined in a logical order. However, the inferences involved in intuition are immediate, without reference to general rules. Intuition gives us a love of God and personal freedom. Those who have

this third type of knowledge naturally understand the way in which things follow from the nature of God and are less subject to passive emotions or passions.

Emotions

In Part III of the Ethics, Spinoza develops a theory of the emotions. He defines emotions as a modification of the body that either increases or decreases its active power. This idea needs explanation. Spinoza claims that everything endeavors to preserve its own being (cf. Hobbes). It has *conatus*, which is like an active power or force towards self-preservation III, 6). This constitutes the essence of the thing in question (III, 7). Therefore, the essence of the human body is its *conatus*, which manifests itself as desires, which are directed towards pleasure and the avoidance of pain (III, 28). In this sense, all desires follow from the necessity of our own nature and in this way, they are naturally good. On this basis, Spinoza defines a passion as an emotion that decreases the active power of the body. It is passive.

Given that all desires follow from our active nature, how do such passive emotions arise? In answer, Spinoza makes two claims. First, because of the theory of conatus, painful things happen to us because of external and not internal causes. Second, passive emotional states or passions arise only from inadequate ideas (III, 3). In other words, passions such as anger, fear, and hatred, occur because of ignorance or incomplete understanding of their external causes. Therefore, in so far as we have an adequate idea of our emotions and their causes, we will not be subject to passions.

Bondage and Freedom

In Book IV of the *Ethics*, 'Of Human Bondage,' Spinoza describes how we enslave ourselves by our attachment to and inadequate understanding of the passions. For example, false piety and political power are based on fear.

However, in Book V, 'Of Human Liberty,' Spinoza develops a positive theory of human freedom. He attempts to oppose freedom to constraint rather than to necessity. To act freely is not to act from an uncaused mental decision, but to act from the necessity of one's own nature. Human freedom resides in the power of the mind to control the passions by having an adequate idea of their external cause. Therefore, as our understanding of Nature grows, the passions will have less control over us. In the grip of the passions, we appear to be under the power of external forces; but, as soon as we form a clear and distinct idea of a passion, it ceases to be one, and we are freed. In this way, a clear understanding that all things are necessary gives the mind power over the passions. At the same time, this allows us to feel the active emotions, such as love. The result is inevitably a greater feeling of pleasure because, by the nature of conatus, we naturally desire pleasure.

This process of liberation involves referring our ideas to the idea of God or Nature as a whole, because the more we understand particular things, the more we understand God (V, 24). Thus, this understanding, which liberates us from the bondage of the passions, instills in us an intellectual love of God, which is the inevitable result of the intuitive knowledge of God.

Conclusion

Spinoza presents us with an unorthodox alternative to Descartes' dualistic attempt to unify science and religion. Spinoza's arguments highlight some of the problems with Descartes' mind/body and God/world dualisms, which according to Spinoza threaten the integrity of the physical sciences. For this reason, Spinoza's metaphysics appears to be a more logical application of the axioms inherent in Descartes' philosophy, namely the Principle of Sufficient Reason and the definition of substance. If substance is by definition independent, and if all causes contain their effects, then substances cannot interact causally. Each substance must be like a universe onto itself, and this apparently supports the conclusion that there can only be one substance.

Spinoza also presents us with an alternative and more ethical vision of human progress than that of Bacon. Scientific progress alone cannot ensure human freedom because freedom must involve liberation from the negative passions that prevent us from feeling natural love. At the same time, Spinoza's ethics is based on the metaphysics of Nature rather than on divine commands and the authority of scripture.

Like Descartes, Spinoza attempts to offer us a metaphysical vision that shows why science and religion are compatible, but Spinoza's conception is less acceptable to the orthodox religious traditions than even Descartes'.

9

Newton: The Grand Vision

Sir Isaac Newton (1642-1727) was born near Lincoln in England, the same year that Galileo died. In 1661, he entered Trinity College Cambridge to study and, in 1665, to teach mathematics and physics. He was elected Professor of Mathematics in 1669. In 1666, the year of the Great Fire of London and the outbreak of the bubonic plague, Newton made three extraordinary discoveries, the first of which was his most famous mathematical breakthrough, the calculus, also found independently by Leibniz. That year, he also discovered that sunlight is composed of light of the colors of the rainbow, each with a specific angle of refraction, which can be separated by a prism. As a result, he developed a corpuscular theory of light, whose velocity he calculated as 190,000 miles per second. His *Opticks* was published in 1704. Also in 1666, Newton made his first formulations of his theory of gravity.

Newton belonged to a generation of British scientists, who were influenced by Bacon's concept of eliminative induction and by Pierre Gassendi's atomism, as well as by the work of Galileo, Descartes and Hobbes. The other prominent member of this circle was the chemist Robert Boyle (1627-91), who defended the principles of mechanist and corpuscular science and formed the Royal Society in 1660, which Newton later presided. In his book *The Origin of Forms and Qualities According to the Corpuscular Theory* (1666), Boyle explains the corpuscular theory, distinguishes primary and secondary qualities, and shows how the theory can explain detailed chemical observations made by Boyle himself. As we saw in Chapters 4 and 7, mechanical science requires only the concept of matter in motion. Newton radically altered this mechanical conception with his theory of gravity.

Gravity

In 1666, Newton began to think of the gravity of the earth extending to the orbit of the moon and, thus, he started to conceive gravity as a universal force between any two bodies with mass. Voltaire portrays Newton as discovering gravity after seeing an apple fall from a tree. The story is probably false. Between 1679 and 1684, Newton worked on the mathematical details of his theory of gravity, using the work of Kepler and Brahe. He formulated the universal law of gravity. The force of gravitational attraction between two bodies varies inversely with the square of the distance between them and directly as the product of their masses, or $F= G\ Mm/d^2$ where 'd' is the distance between the two bodies and G is the gravitational constant. He showed how this law explains the elliptical orbits of the planets around the sun, as described by Kepler and explains the rate at which bodies fall towards the earth.

Although Newton generally embraced a mechanical view of explanation, the force of gravity is an exception. In his system, gravity is a genuine action at a distance. In other words, one body directly and immediately affects another distant body without any intervening physical mechanism or contact. Newton was aware that his conception of gravity contradicted the principles of mechanistic science, and, although he professed agnosticism as to whether gravity was a material or immaterial agency, he probably conceived it as immaterial and direct manifestation of God.

Indeed, Newton believed that God was co-extensive with the infinite material universe as a whole because absolute space and time have divine-like features. An absolute conception of space affirms that space is a real infinite entity that is logically prior to the matter that may or may not occupy it. This is a view that Leibniz disputes by arguing for a purely relational theory of space and time (see Chapter 13). Newton contends that the existence of absolute space and time is required to explain absolute motion, which is motion with respect to absolute space for a period of absolute time. Uniform motion in a straight line is purely relative. In other words, the uniform rectilinear movement of body A compared to body B may be equally well considered as the opposite motion of B relative to A. However, Newton argues that non-uniform and non-rectilinear motions, such as acceleration and rotation, must be considered as absolute and, therefore, that they require the existence of absolute space and time. Newton affirms that God, who exists everywhere and at all times, constitutes space and time, which as infinite entities may be considered as manifestations of God. In brief, Newton does not conceive the universe as a mechanical system, as is sometimes thought.

The Principia

Newton's *Principia*, published in 1687, is one of the most important scientific works of all time, In this work, Newton lays down his three laws of motion. The first law states that every body continues in its state of rest, or uniform motion in a straight line, unless it is moved to change that state by external forces. The second law states that the change of motion is proportional to the external force and is made in the direction of the straight line in which that force is applied. The third law states that for every action there is an equal and opposite reaction. Newton shows how these three laws, together with the principle of gravity, explain a huge variety of natural phenomena, extending from the orbits of the planets to the relative density of the earth, and from the force of the tides to the flattening of the earth at the poles.

In the second edition of the *Principia*, Newton lays out his philosophy of science, which consists in a combination of rigorous experimentation, mathematical laws and a minimum theoretical commitment. In other words, scientists should frame general hypotheses in mathematical terms based on specific observations and should subject those hypotheses to experimentation. Newton was firmly opposed to speculative hypotheses and argued that any hypothesis concerning the cause of phenomena should be subject to independent empirical testing.

Newton's physics had its critics. Leibniz, Berkeley and, later, Kant criticized Newton's assumption that space and time are absolute. Leibniz also criticized Newton's idea of gravity as an action at a distance, without any intervening causal mechanism. Nevertheless, the earlier promise of natural science to explain the workings of the universe with a few simple principles seemed to be fulfilled by Newton's comprehensive scientific vision. Eventually, Newton's physics usurped the dominance in Europe of Descartes' mechanics. It remained the physical paradigm until Einstein's theories of special and general relativity in the early twentieth century. After Newton died at the age of 85, Voltaire marveled that a mathematician was buried with the honors usually reserved for kings.

10

Locke and the Proper Business

John Locke (1632–1704) lived during a time of many changes. The year he was born, 1632, Galileo published his critique of the claim that the earth is the still center of the universe. Five years later, Descartes published the *Discourse on A Method*. The intellectual climate of Europe was changing. Scholastic medieval philosophy was being replaced by the new science, developed by, among others, Locke's friends, such as Newton and Boyle. This was an exciting intellectual revolution.

It was also a period of political transformation in Britain. After seven years of Civil War, England became a republic in 1649, when Locke was 17. Eleven years later, England reverted to a monarchy. However, soon Protestant England was unhappy with the new Catholic king and, in 1689, King James II, was replaced by the Protestant monarchs William and Mary. Locke was an important activist in this peaceful "revolution," which marked the end of absolute monarchy in Britain.

These political changes were intermingled with religious tensions throughout Europe. In 1648, the Thirty Years' War ended leaving Germany destroyed. Catholic France was the major power on the continent, and it was dominated by the Sun King, Louis XIV, who seemed ready to invade Protestant Netherlands. During this time of religious strife, Locke was a champion of toleration.

Locke was an active participant in the scientific, political and religious changes in the society of his time, but he was also a thinker who reflected on the meaning of these changes. He saw the need to avoid the extremes of fanatical enthusiasm on the one hand, and pessimistic skepticism, on the other. He was against authoritarianism, dogma, and the repression of individual free thought. Above all, Locke was concerned to reveal the importance of morality as a force for freedom in both politics and religion.

An Exciting Life of Moderation

Locke composed his own epitaph in which he describes himself 'as contented with his modest lot. A scholar by training he devoted his studies wholly to the pursuit of truth.' Despite his temperament of moderation, Locke had a very exciting life. A doctor, he worked with the famous scientists of the time and, because of his political activities, he had to flee the country for fear of his life. He was a scholar, thinker and writer whose work became famous and influential during his own lifetime.

Locke finished his university degree in 1656 at Christ Church College, Oxford. During this early stage of his life, however, his main interest was medicine, which he studied unofficially, but in earnest in the late 1650's. In 1660, Locke met Robert Boyle, the famous chemist and founder of the Royal Society. Locke became an active member of a group of young scientists centered around Boyle, who were interested in practicing the new experimental method.

During the summer of 1666, Locke met Lord Ashley, the Chancellor of the Exchequer, and who later became the Earl of Shaftesbury and Lord Chancellor of England, who was also a philosopher. Locke became his secretary and physician, and he moved to London where he became actively involved in politics. At this time, Locke formed a discussion group and, as a result of this, in 1671, he started work on a manuscript which was later to become the *Essay Concerning Human Understanding*. He also wrote works on medicine, economics and on religious toleration.

Towards the end of 1675, Locke left England for France for three and half years for a rest needed because of his bronchial problems. When Locke returned to England, the country was once again in the grip of political unrest. King Charles II and his brother James were both staunch Catholics, but the majority of the people of England were Protestant. Shaftesbury had become the leader of the opposition and became involved in plots to remove the king. In 1681, Shaftesbury was arrested on a charge of high treason and spent a few months in the Tower before being acquitted. In 1683, Locke fled to Holland.

During his five-year exile in Holland, Locke had the time to write. His letters concerning education were later published as *Some Thoughts Concerning Education* (1693). He also wrote about toleration and worked on his *Essay Concerning Human Understanding*. Meanwhile, he became involved once again in revolutionary politics. The opposition in England was planning to replace King James II with Prince William of Holland and his wife Mary (James's daughter). Locke became an advisor to William and Mary in Rotterdam.

In early 1689, William and Mary peacefully replaced James II on the English throne and Locke returned to England. He was now fifty-six years old. He was soon to become a figure of national fame, because of three major publications. In 1689, his *Letter Concerning Toleration* and *Two Treatises on Civil Government* were published. In 1690, his most famous work, the *Essay Concerning Human Understanding*, also appeared.

The Essay

Locke wrote two drafts of the *Essay* in 1671 and a third in 1685. The first edition of the book was published in 1690. Before examining the details of the *Essay*, it is important to understand the context, aim, and conclusion of the work,

The context is that, in early 1671, Locke and a group of friends met to discuss the nature of morality and religion. During these discussions, Locke suggested a new line of inquiry: the limits of human knowledge, and the group asked him to prepare a paper on the topic, which became the *Essay*.

Locke's main avowed aim in the *Essay* is to discover the nature and limits of human knowledge, especially of the new sciences, which were championed by his friends Newton and Boyle, and which were growing in confidence. In other words, Locke wanted to present both the foundations of natural science and, at the same time, evaluate the claim that modern science will give us knowledge of the universe.

Locke's conclusion about science is surprisingly cautious and skeptical. Science can only yield probable opinion and not knowledge. Moreover, in contrast, Locke thinks that knowledge of morality is possible. He argues that moral knowledge can be demonstrated and, therefore, can be known with certainty. Towards the end of the *Essay*, he claims: 'Hence, I think I may conclude that morality is the proper science and business of mankind in general' (IV.III.11).

Locke reaches these general conclusions in three steps:

1) First, he tries to show that all ideas are derived from experience. He shows this first, by arguing against innate ideas and, second, by

showing how certain key concepts are derived from experience. This argument is contained in Books I and II of the *Essay*.

2) Second, he argues that, because meaningful words directly stand for ideas rather than properties of objects, we cannot hope to gain knowledge of the real essences of things upon which science depends. This argument is contained in Book III of the *Essay*.

3) Finally, in Book IV, he defines knowledge as a relation between ideas that requires certainty. A belief can count as knowledge only if one can be certain that it is true. Locke argues that science can only offer us beliefs that are probably true.

In summary, Locke's work is a two edged sword. On the one hand, he uses his Empiricist account of the origin of our ideas to argue against scholastic notions and to develop the concepts necessary for science. On the other hand, he uses those same tools to argue against the possibility of scientific knowledge. This, however, does not amount to skepticism because he argues that science can give us opinions or beliefs that are probably true.

The New Way of Ideas

Locke calls his philosophical approach 'the new way of ideas.' Ideas are the immediate objects of perception and thought. Locke says:

> Whatsoever the mind perceives in itself or is the immediate object of perception, thought or understanding, that I call 'idea'. (I,i,8)

Ideas exist only as the objects of cognitive mental activities, such as thought and perception. They do not exist apart from such activities. Furthermore, thought and perception always must be of something and, according to Locke, this something is always an idea in the mind. Whenever we perceive or think, the immediate object of perception is an idea, and the idea is essential to the identity of the thought or perception. If a person were thinking about something else, then he or she would not be having the same thought.

What is the new way of ideas? Locke's theory is that all ideas are derived from experience. He shows this first, by arguing against innate ideas, and second, by showing in detail how our ideas are derived from experience. Locke uses this explanation of the origin of ideas to give a theory of knowledge that allows him to evaluate the prospects of science and to find a firmer basis for morality and religion by rejecting dogma.

Book I of the *Essay* is a sustained attack on the doctrine of innate ideas, which had powerful religious and political implications. Innate ideas were assumed to be God given, and the appeal to innate ideas was an authoritarian argument. Innate ideas could not be challenged. Consequently, Locke's argument against innate ideas is an attempt to liberate epistemology from dogma and authority. Furthermore, by showing that ideas are not innate, Locke supports his own positive claim that they are all derived from sensory experience. Locke's basic argument for rejecting innate ideas is his definition of 'idea' as the immediate object of perception. Because of this, Locke claims that the notion of innate ideas is absurd; such a notion implies that we have some ideas of which we are not conscious.

However, he also tries to reply to arguments in favor of innate ideas. He notes that one such argument is that certain principles are universally held to be true. For example, the claim that parents have an obligation to care for their children seems so obvious that anyone who understands the words will agree with it. This might be thought to be proof that such principles are inherent in our understanding. Against such an argument, Locke claims that the universal acceptance of a principle does not mean that it is innate. It must be shown that the principle could not be known in any other way. Locke claims that this could not be demonstrated because there are universally accepted principles that are clearly not innate, such as 'The color white is not black' (I,ii,18).

Book II consists of a long argument for the conclusion that all ideas come from sensation and reflection. The essence of Locke's theory of ideas is that all simple ideas come from sensation or reflection, and that all complex ideas come from the operation of our minds on those simple ideas. This means that all ideas originate in sensation and reflection. The mind generates complex ideas from simple ones by uniting, repeating and comparing them. It can do this in an indefinite number of ways. This is how we produce ideas of monsters and of things that we have never seen.

While the mind actively constructs complex ideas, it passively receives simple ideas in experience. Locke argues that the mind is incapable of inventing new simple ideas and is restricted to those it passively receives in experience. It is just as impossible for the mind to construct or invent new simple ideas as it is for a blind person to have ideas of color.

To be able to defend systematically the claim that all ideas originate in experience, Locke classifies complex ideas according to the mental operations that compose them. Locke gives a three-fold classification of complex ideas:

- When ideas are compounded, they form the idea of substances and modes.
- When simple ideas are compared, they become the idea of relations.
- General ideas result from the mental operation of abstraction.

Locke's discussion of the complex ideas of substances, modes and relations is the backbone of Book II of the *Essay*.

Primary and Secondary Qualities

Before examining complex ideas, we need to discuss Locke's theory of perception and his distinction between primary and secondary qualities. This distinction has two parts.

First, primary qualities, such as solidity, shape, extension, motion, and number, are the intrinsic properties of all material things. In contrast, secondary qualities, such as colors, tastes, sounds, and smells, are simply the power of objects to produce certain ideas in us. These secondary qualities are based on the primary qualities of the minute particles. For example, color is simply the arrangement of these particles, and this is the basis of the power of that object to cause in us the sensation of color.

Second, the ideas of primary qualities resemble primary qualities themselves, but the ideas of secondary qualities resemble nothing in the object. Our ideas of colors and the like do not resemble the primary qualities of minute particles.

This distinction results from applying the corpuscular theory of matter to perception. We should explain perception in terms of the action of corpuscles on our sensory organs, because this is the only way that objects can affect our sense organs. In other words, Locke's main argument for his distinction is that the corpuscular theory of science is sufficient to explain the causal mechanisms of perception and that this theory gives us no reason for believing that our ideas of secondary qualities resemble qualities in objects.

We need to set these points in the context of Locke's representationalist theory of perception, according to which we can know external objects only indirectly, by directly experiencing the ideas that represent them. According to this theory, we directly perceive ideas in our own minds, and these ideas can represent the objects in the external world that are the cause of the ideas. So, Locke argues that the fact that our ideas do represent those objects permits us to claim that we perceive external objects indirectly.

Locke's theory may look like common sense. However, it faces a problem, namely: how we can ever know anything about external objects when we only ever directly perceive our own ideas? In particular, how is it ever possible to know that our ideas sometimes resemble external objects? Locke himself recognizes these problems, which were inherent in Descartes' method of doubt.

Locke responds in four ways. First, he notes that our perceptual ideas are not under the direct control of our will. We do not produce them and, consequently, it is reasonable to think that they are caused by external objects. Second, the different senses corroborate one another. Together they testify as to the nature of external things with regard to primary qualities. Third, Locke dismisses skepticism. It would be unreasonable to expect more evidence than that provided by our senses. For example, it is a mistake to expect a logical demonstration of the existence of external objects. Such things cannot be known with complete certainty. Furthermore, we do not need additional evidence. The senses provide all the evidence we require for the practical concerns of everyday life. Fourth, Locke concedes that we are utterly ignorant of the way ideas are caused by external objects. In general, he claims that the connection between matter and mind is incomprehensible. As we shall see, this last point is of great importance in Locke's overall philosophy because it places a general limit on scientific knowledge.

We might wonder whether Locke's replies to skepticism are adequate. First, Descartes thinks that skeptical arguments need to be answered and tries takes up the challenge. Can Locke adequately reply to the argument of Descartes' third stage of doubt? Second, Berkeley and Hume both argue that Locke's position implies a certain skepticism, even though Locke does not realize it.

The Three Kinds of Complex Ideas

To return to the main point, as we have seen, Locke divides complex ideas into three categories: ideas of modes, ideas of substances, and ideas of relations. To maintain his empiricist theory, Locke must argue that all complex ideas can be derived from simple ideas. He does this case by case.

a) Modes

Modes depend on the existence of substances, which can exist by themselves. Locke subdivides modes into simple and mixed ones. Simple modes are combinations of the same idea. They result from the operations of combining simple ideas of the same kind and include our ideas of space, time, number, and infinity. Our ideas of mixed modes originate in the combination of simple ideas of different kinds; examples of such mixed modes are triumph, murder, and drunkenness.

b) Substance in General

In Chapter 23 of Book II, Locke attacks the notion of substance, which is important to thinkers such as Descartes and Spinoza. Locke begins his attack by distinguishing three types of ideas concerning substance:

1. The idea of particular substances or objects, such as the idea of the sun;
2. The idea of different kinds of substances, such as the ideas of gold, lead, or oxygen;
3. The abstract idea of substance in general.

Locke thinks that this final abstract idea is problematic. He explains it as follows (II.XXIII.1). Consider an individual object such as a cup, which has many properties or qualities. Because these qualities are universals, while the cup itself is a particular, the cup must be distinct from each and all of its properties. However, properties cannot exist by themselves; they must inhere in something. For this reason, we posit the notion of a substratum in which the properties inhere and which is itself distinct from them. In this way, we assume that the general idea of substance requires the concept of a pure substratum. Substance so conceived is property-less. It has no positive nature and, therefore, it cannot be identified with any specific kind of substance, such as silver.

Locke rejects this notion of substratum. He says that we cannot acquire such an idea by sensation or reflection, and he calls the idea confused, and claims that if any idea had to be innate, it would be this one (II, XIII, 19). By rejecting the idea of pure substratum, he disarms its philosophical use.

c) Relations: Causality and Identity

Our ideas of relations arise from the mental act of comparing ideas and thus originate from simple ideas (II.XXV.9). To show this, Locke examines the relational ideas of cause and identity. The notion of cause is important for Locke's theory, for example, when he speaks of secondary qualities as causal powers. Almost anticipating and replying to Hume's later skepticism about the idea of causation, Locke argues that the concept of a causal power can be derived from experience. He suggests that the idea of causation is not derived from sense experience alone, but also from introspection or reflection. By reflection, we discover that we can move our arms (or other parts of our bodies) merely by willing them to move. Locke claims that we derive the idea of active causal power from the experience of our own will. This point is important because Hume later argues that our normal conception of causation cannot be derived from experience.

In Chapter 27, Locke examines the identity relation. He claims that identity is a special kind of relation because the conditions for identity vary according to the nature of the thing in question (II.xxvii.7). For example, simple material bodies can be identified on the basis of their spatial position at a given time. The identity of living creatures depends on their organization, which determines a common life. Hence, the identity of an oak tree is not changed because it grows.

Locke distinguishes between the concepts of a human being and of a person. A person is a rational, self-conscious being. The concept of person carries implications of responsibility for actions. If A is the same person as B, then B is responsible for the actions of A. In contrast, a human being is an animal of a certain form.

According to Locke, the identity of persons depends on the continuity of consciousness through time. A self X is the same person as an earlier self Y when X's present memory of the past is the result of Y's consciousness of what was at that time present. I am the same person as I was ten years ago, because my present memories of ten years ago are the result of my experiences then.

Locke argues against two opposing views of personal identity. First, he objects to the continuity of body as a criterion of personal identity. We can imagine that two distinct persons might inhabit the same body—one by day, and the other by night. Conversely, we could imagine the same consciousness acting in two distinct bodies, which would amount to the same person having two bodies. Moreover, the same consciousness might be passed from body to body; thus, the consciousness and memories of a prince might enter the body of a cobbler, and vice versa. For these reasons, personal identity cannot be constituted by the continuity of bodily substance.

Second, he argues against the identity of the soul as a criterion of personal identity. The same person could have two souls and, conversely, two persons could have the same soul. Even if the soul of Socrates was reincarnated as the present Mayor of Queenborough, they would not be the same person, unless the mayor had direct consciousness 'from the inside' of the experiences of Socrates. If the same soul has two alternating and distinct sets of conscious thoughts and experiences, then in effect two alternating persons would share the same soul. For these reasons, personal identity cannot be constituted by the continuity of a soul substance.

Note that Locke is agnostic regarding the mind/body problem. He does not argue for dualism or for materialism. He does not deny that there are mental substances, but neither does he deny that the mind might be a configuration of matter, or that matter thinks. Locke argues for this radical claim in two ways. First, he thinks that the notion of substance in general is that of something unknowable. This would apply just as much to the idea of a non-material substance, as it does to material substance. If there were a non-material mind, it would be unknowable. Second, Locke rejects the idea that our personal identity consists in the identity of a non-material substance. In other words, he rejects the claim that personal identity requires the existence of a non-material mind or soul.

Against Real Essences

Book III examines the relations between words and ideas, and the nature of classification. Locke repudiates the scholastic idea that the essences of natural kinds can be grasped by reasoning from definitions. This view involves a misunderstanding of language and definition. According to Locke, words stand for ideas in the mind of the person who uses them (III.I.2). Words stand directly for ideas, rather than for the properties of things, because we know directly only our own ideas. Communication is possible because certain words have become associated with particular ideas 'by long and familiar use.' Particular words stand for specific ideas (III.I.8). Thus, one person understands another when the ideas that the first person has while uttering the words excite in the other person the same ideas. Thus, the purpose of definition is to make these ideas clear.

Locke argues that definitions do not determine real essences or Platonic forms. In Chapter III, he says that a language must contain general words, which make comparisons and generalizations. However, general words do not name universal entities, such as Plato's forms, because only particulars exist. Instead, general words name general ideas. General words, such as 'red,' stand for general ideas in our minds, rather than universal Platonic forms. We acquire general ideas by abstraction. For instance, by attending selectively to the quality that a group of round things have in common, we acquire the general notion of roundness. In this way, Locke tries to provide an empiricist account of the formation of general ideas and the meaning of general words.

Locke has another reason for rejecting the Platonic picture: it assumes that we can know the essential natures common to all things of one kind. He rejects this assumption by distinguishing between real and nominal essence. The nominal essence of a substance type, such as gold, is an abstract idea of something having certain characteristics. We classify an object as a piece of gold because of its yellow shining color, its weight, and so on. We associate this complex idea with the name 'gold.' The complex idea is formed by abstraction.

In contrast, the real essence of gold is its internal constitution, which is generally unknown. The observable characteristics of gold causally depend on the real essence of gold, which provides a scientific basis for its observable properties.

However, the real essences of things is unknown. Hence, they do not constitute the actual basis of our classifications, which depend on nominal essences. Since the nominal essence is an abstract idea of the mind, it will involve a conventional element. It is to some extent arbitrary because it depends on the selections made by our attention. On the other hand, Locke admits that things really do resemble one another and that our classifications have some basis in these real similarities, and thus they are not entirely arbitrary. Nevertheless, words do not refer to the real essence of things. General words can only signify ideas.

Locke says that a failure to distinguish between real and nominal essence leads to a false view of knowledge. Disputing definitions is a fruitless method of inquiry, because definitions only determine nominal essences. In this way, Locke denies that we can have a priori knowledge of the world. In contrast, the primary purpose of definition is to clarify what idea a word stands for. Words can stand for unclear ideas or for several ideas at once. The purpose of definition is to remedy these abuses of language and make communication clearer. Definitions do not provide a priori knowledge of real essences.

Knowledge

In Book IV Locke discusses the nature of knowledge, which has three features. First, it entails making judgments. Merely having an idea is not the same as judging that idea to be true or false. Second, knowledge requires certainty and justification. Beliefs that are merely probable do not count as knowledge (IV.III.14). Third, Locke defines knowledge as the perception of certain relations of agreement and disagreement between our ideas (IV.I.1). Knowledge is confined to ideas. In Chapter I of Book IV, Locke lists four sorts of agreement and disagreement. The first two clearly fit Locke's definition of knowledge but the final two are more problematic.

1. Identity and Diversity: This type of knowledge is expressed by 'trifling propositions,' such as 'Red is red' which merely require the judgment that an idea is what it is.

2. Logical Relations: This kind of knowledge is obtained by judging the logical relations between ideas. It is expressed with propositions such as 'The angles of a triangle equal 180 degrees.' This kind of knowledge can be found in ethics, politics, and religion

(IV.III.18), and Locke considers it the most extensive kind of knowledge.

3. Coexistence: There are regularities in our ideas. Our knowledge of physical objects consists in the judgment that the ideas of certain qualities accompany each other or belong together. For example, knowledge of gold consists in the judgment that the ideas of yellowness, weight, and certain powers always accompany each other.

4. Real Existence: At IV.1.7, Locke says that the fourth relation is 'that of the actual real existence agreeing to any idea.'

In Chapter II of Book IV, Locke describes three different degrees of knowledge. Intuitive knowledge is an immediate perception of agreement between ideas, which leaves no room for doubt, e.g. 'three is greater than two.' Demonstrative knowledge requires intervening steps, as in a mathematical or logical proof. Sensitive knowledge of particular external objects through the senses is even less certain than demonstrative knowledge (IV.II.14

Although Locke thinks that sensitive knowledge is possible, his definition of knowledge casts a pessimistic shadow on the hope that science will enlarge our knowledge of nature. He does not doubt that scientific progress will be useful, but he contends that we should be content with probable belief and opinion rather than insisting on true knowledge, since 'our faculties are not fitted to penetrate into the internal fabric and real essences of bodies' (IV.XII.11).

Locke sharply contrasts the gloomy prospects for scientific knowledge with those for morality. Locke argues that moral knowledge can be demonstrated and therefore can be known with certainty.

Ethics

Morality was one of Locke's main philosophical concerns. However, he never wrote a systematic work on ethics, although he planned to do so. Nevertheless, the *Essay* contains some indications of Locke's views, and these are an important preliminary to his political views, which we shall examine in the next chapter.

Although Locke denies that science can give us knowledge, he argues that moral knowledge is possible. He argues this on the basis of important similarities between mathematics and ethics. First, morality concerns the necessary connections between abstract ideas, and in this way it is like mathematics. Second, both morals and mathematics deal with abstract objects, which are really modes. In both cases, there is no difference between real and nominal essence, and therefore, no possibility of ignorance on these grounds. In this way, mathematics and morality are different from the natural sciences in which real and nominal essence diverge. Third, both morality and mathematics are prior to experience in the sense that in both we can gain knowledge by deduction or intuition without appeal to sense-experience. We can know a priori that murder is wrong, without knowing whether a murder has been committed. Because of these similarities, Locke is convinced that morality can be made into a deductive science.

Three Characterizations of Morality

Locke gives us three schematic characterizations of morality. He also implies that they are three aspects of the same point.

1) Natural Law

A law holds for all human beings independently of all institutions. Such laws are knowable by reason. Locke usually calls these laws, the laws of nature or the natural law. Such phrases refer to the basic rules that govern the universe, but they also include the moral rules to which all rational beings should conform their actions.

Locke denies the idea of innate moral knowledge. This makes his view different from the traditional natural law theories that assert that conscience is innate knowledge of moral principles. In contrast, Locke argues that conscience is merely the moral opinion of one's own actions, and such opinions may be derived from education or custom (I,iii,8). Furthermore, he argues that the innateness hypothesis is incompatible with the role of reason in morality. Of any practical principle, we can ask what is the reason for it? This would not be so if principles were innate. Locke's view is that God intended us to think for ourselves and, for this reason, He gave us innate capacities, and not innate ideas and knowledge.

2) God's Will

According to Locke, being moral consists in following God's law. Locke argues that the concept of obligation requires the idea of law, which in turn requires the idea of a lawmaker. In short, morality consists of laws. Laws are rules that are commanded by someone who has the power to enforce them with punishment. For this reason, the idea of moral obligation requires the existence of God who commands such laws.

3) Pleasure

Locke claims that the good is whatever produces pleasure. 'Pleasure' for Locke, refers to what a person desires or prefers. Locke affirms that people desire very different things (II,xxi,55). As a consequence, he denies the usefulness of the ancient question: 'What way of living is the good life for a human being?'

Locke holds that doing harm to a community is worse than doing a harm against an individual. On the basis of this, we may suppose that Locke would have claimed that an act that promotes more happiness for more people would be better than one which secures less happiness for fewer people.

Locke explains moral beliefs in terms of pleasure and pain in order to show how moral ideas fit into his overall empiricist framework. The concepts of good and bad are derived from our ideas of pleasure and pain. In other words, we do not need to postulate a different or special faculty to explain the origin of moral concepts. They, like all other ideas, are acquired from experience.

Furthermore, Locke embraces a hedonist view of human motivation, according to which all our actions are motivated ultimately by the prospect of pleasure and the avoidance of pain. (II, xxi, 41) This does not exclude the happiness of others being part of one's own happiness. In this way, it is not necessarily an egoistic view. However, given such a view, it is understandable why Locke thinks that we can only make sense of the concepts of goodness and badness in terms of pleasure and pain.

The Unity of the Three

We have briefly examined Locke's three characterizations of morality. How does he reconcile them? The following quotation encapsulates his overarching idea:

> What duty is cannot be understood without a law; nor a law be known or supposed without a law-maker, or without reward and punishment. (I,iii,12)

The first point is that the laws of nature themselves come from God. In this way, Locke reconciles reason and religion. Reason tells us that we should follow the natural law. However, those same laws are divinely commanded. Consequently, the dictates of reason do not conflict with the commands of God. God does not will arbitrarily and, therefore, He commands acts that are rational.

The second point is that something morally good produces a pleasure that is a reward from God. God attaches pleasure to certain kinds of acts, in order to reward us for obeying His laws. Through reason we can learn what God wills, for what God wills conforms to the laws of nature or the moral law. This is the rational ground of morality. What we might call the motivational ground of morality is pleasure. God backs up his laws with sanctions and rewards, or pain and pleasure, because we are subject to weakness of the will.

In summary, Locke's idea of morality is that an act is morally good if it complies with the laws of reason, which are also commanded by God, and which God enforces with reward and punishment, through pleasure and pain. (II,xxviii, 5).

Although Locke thinks that our knowledge of right and wrong are derived from reasoning, he also thinks that revealed scripture is an important source of our understanding of morality. He claims that God created all persons free and equal. Consequently, the laws of nature affirm the natural equality of all persons and, on the basis of this, we have certain natural rights, including the right to freedom and ownership. These in turn are vital elements in Locke's political theory

11

Locke: A Reasonable Revolutionary

Locke was born into a turbulent age. In 1642, when he was 10 years old, Civil War broke out in England. Locke's father fought in the Parliamentary army against the Royalists. In 1649, King Charles I was executed, and England became a republic for eleven years, until 1660 when Charles II was crowned king. The violence of this period had a profound effect on Locke's outlook. His work rejects the mad passion and zeal of the Civil War and, instead, it reflects a reasonable and carefully balanced attitude to life. It illustrates the virtues of serious reflection, very much in keeping with the spirit of the new generation, which spurned the emotionalism of the Civil War. In this vein, Locke argues for religious toleration, for an eminently reasonable version of Christianity, and for a balanced form of government to replace the excesses of absolute monarchy.

A Peaceful Revolution

In 1679, less than twenty years after the restoration of Charles II, the political situation in England was threatening to become unstable again. The legitimate heir to the throne was James, the younger brother of Charles II. James was a Catholic and there were strong fears that he would try to impose his religion on the country. After Charles' death in 1685, James II become king and, true to expectations, he began imposing Catholicism on England. Furthermore, he believed in absolute monarchy. As a result, James was a very unpopular ruler and the opposition in England was planning to install Prince William of Orange of Holland on the English throne, on the basis that he was the Protestant husband of Mary, the legitimate daughter of James II. In 1687, Locke moved to Rotterdam to advise Prince William. In April 1688 William decided that he would support the opposition to King James and he began to prepare his campaign to take the throne. In November 1688, he set sail for England.

The English people welcomed the Protestant prince and the king's daughter. Towns surrendered without a shot. James had no real support. He fled to France and William of Orange entered London and he and Mary were proclaimed king and queen in February 1689.

These dramatic events ignited powerful political debates. Locke's great political work, the *Two Treatises on Government,* primarily justifies the right to resist an unjust authority. It contains a justification of revolution against absolute monarchy. Consequently, its publication in August 1689 was very apt. In fact, Locke had written the majority of the manuscript before he left for Holland in 1683, at the time when he was serving Shaftesbury.

The Political Theory

Locke's political theory consists of three main elements:
1) The criticism of the claim that kings have a divine right to rule.
2) The theory of consent that gives governments' their legitimacy.
3) The theory of property, which shows how a person can acquire the right to own private property.

1) Against Divine Rights

Locke's first treatise tries to refute the claims of Sir Robert Filmer who argued that the right of kings to rule over their subjects was divine or based on the authority of God. In reply to Filmer, Locke's main argument is that the basis of political power is a social contract, which establishes a civil society governed by laws.

2) The Theory of Consent

According to Locke, in the state of nature, prior to the formation of any civil society, people obey the moral laws only insofar as they happen to be rational. In the state of nature, any person may punish any other for acting immorally according to his or her judgment of what is immoral. The state of nature is, therefore, unstable and insecure. Common agreement about the enforcement of morality is needed for people to live together in a more secure environment. To live securely, people need openly stated and commonly known expectations of each other, which require laws enforced by a political power. Furthermore, such laws are required for the sake of our prosperity, because property rights can be upheld with security and peace only with public and enforceable laws.

The social contract is an agreement between individuals to form a society according to which they give up their right to enforce morality over to a government, in order to gain security for themselves and their property. This analysis of the origin of society shows the purpose of government. It is for the mutual preservation of life, liberty and property. From this, it follows that government should not control and rule. It should serve. It also follows that the individual should give up his or her rights to the minimum degree necessary for the mutual protection of the members of society.

3) The Theory of Property

Locke also tries to explain how individual property rights can be justified. How can the idea of humanity as a whole receiving God's gift be compatible with individual private property? The essence of Locke's answer is labor. Labor belongs to the person who works. By applying labor to raw materials and other unowned things, a person can make those things his or her private property. In other words, the person acquires private property rights over land, minerals and energy through his or her work.

We have a God-given right to freedom of action and this is the basis of the claim that each person has a right to their own labor and, thereby, the right to own private property. This latter right has important political implications. For example, Locke claims that a monarch cannot legitimately levy taxes on his own authority. He requires the consent of the people or of their legislature. However, according to Locke, property rights are not absolute. They are limited by other moral obligations, such as the duty to not waste and to promote the common or general good.

Economic development necessitates the existence of contracts and property laws to regulate commerce, and such laws require the existence of a government. As the wealth of society increases, leaders are more likely to act in their own self-interest, and so we need to balance the power of the executive with a parliament that represents the people.

Tolerance

With the publication of *Letter Concerning Toleration* (1689), *Two Treatises on Civil Government* (1689) and *Essay Concerning Human Understanding* (1690), Locke was catapulted into fame. He refused political posts offered to him and decided to concentrate on writing. He spent much of his time in the countryside, staying with his friend, the philosopher, Lady Masham. He wrote several works on economics, but his main interest was religion.

In the *Essay*, Locke had argued that the idea of God is acquired through experience, through sensations and reflection, like all the other ideas we have. The idea is acquired by thinking of a being that combines the most desirable qualities in their most perfect form. According to Locke, this implies that we do not have a positive idea of God. For example, God's goodness is perfect; such goodness is beyond our knowledge. This applies to all the qualities of God, and in this way He is incomprehensible.

Nevertheless, in the *Essay,* Locke had argued that the existence of God can be proved. His proof is given at IV, 10, and it consists of two parts. In the first part, Locke proves the existence of God using the principle that everything must have a cause. From this, he argues that only something eternal does not have an external cause. Anything that has a beginning must have an external cause. He concludes that there must be a first cause that is itself eternal, otherwise nothing could be explained, even our own existence. The second part of Locke's proof is to demonstrate the nature of this eternal cause. Locke says that the fact that I am a conscious being shows that the first cause itself must be conscious. Additionally, the order in the universe shows us that the first cause must be intelligent. Furthermore, we are moral beings, and so our ultimate cause must be moral too.

In the *Letter Concerning Toleration,* Locke uses the results of the *Essay* to make a different point. Locke lived during a period when there was a proliferation of different Christian sects in Europe. Lutherans, Calvinists, Anglicans and Catholics were persecuting each other in different countries. In opposition to this climate of intolerance, Locke advocates religious freedom. Mainly he does so on the grounds that the essence of religion is the personal relationship between the individual and God. Such a relationship cannot be regulated institutionally or politically. He advances three central arguments in favor of religious tolerance.

First, churches have no right to punish and persecute because they have no political power. In this sense, a church is not like the state. States are formed when individuals give up the power or right to enforce morality on others, which they entrust to a government. This is why the state does have the power to punish people and execute laws. Churches, on the other hand, are voluntary associations, and are not based on people giving up political power according to a social contract. Therefore, they have no right to prosecute or persecute.

Second, while force and persecution might bring outward conformity, they do not bring inward conviction. Thus, they generate false religion and hypocrisy. People cannot be saved by endorsing religious creeds that they do not really believe. Therefore, religious persecution does not bring about the changes it allegedly seeks.

At the time when Locke was writing, his views were very radical. They appear so much less today, partly because Locke's insistence on the separation of the functions of state and church, and his views on toleration have become largely accepted by our society. To some extent, they have become part of common sense.

Reasonable Christianity

Locke's third argument for religious tolerance is based on a radical redefinition of Christianity. When sects make contradictory claims about doctrinal matters, they cannot all be right. Locke's diagnosis of this situation is that people are making claims that go beyond what they can know. In this way, religious controversy is an epistemological issue, which is answered by the arguments of the *Essay*. Sects arise because people make speculative claims that have no rational support, and religious conflict arises because such speculation becomes dogma.

With this diagnosis, Locke argues that religious tolerance is a requirement of epistemology. By being careful in our judgements about what we know and believe, we will become clearer about what faith requires and what it does not. This clarity will help us to separate dogma and faith. This will promote religious tolerance, which in turn promotes peace and prosperity.

Locke saw that this argument required a redefinition of Christian faith. He distinguishes the doctrines required by a particular church and those that are required by the Bible. According to Locke, the Christianity of the Bible makes two essential demands: first, to believe that Christ is the Messiah sent by God, and second, to live according to Christian morality. Anyone who complies with these two demands is a Christian. In this way, according to Locke, Christianity is a simple and reasonable faith.

So defined, Christianity is a reasonable faith because it does not contradict reason. Even divinely revealed knowledge, which cannot be gained from reason, must accord with reason. In this way, religious knowledge can go beyond reason, but still be reasonable. However, we cannot know for certain that there has been a divine revelation, nor what its message is. Despite this skepticism, revelation is important in religion, because through it, we do not need to have direct evidence for the content of what God reveals, but rather only for the claim that it is or has been revealed to us by Him.

In the face of religious fragmentation, Locke saw his definition of the Christian faith as the only way to defend Christianity as a true religion. He saw the differences between the different Christian sects as unimportant compared to the simple essence of Christianity.

For the period in which he was writing, Locke's theory is a very radical way of understanding Christianity. For example, although Locke does not deny the Trinity, it is not listed among the minimal doctrines of a reasonable Christianity. Locke dedicated the last decade of his life to advocating this position. In 1695, he published The *Reasonableness of Christianity*. He also wrote commentaries on the Epistles of St. Paul, in which he adopted a critical and historical approach to interpreting the Bible.

However, in a way, Locke's underlying concerns during this later period are much the same as they were in the *Essay*. First, much as he did in the *Essay*, in this later period, Locke is arguing once again against authority, and trying to avoid both speculation and skepticism. First and foremost, Locke's concern is morality, which is intimately related to God's commands. Above all, Locke was concerned to reveal the importance of morality as a force for freedom in both politics and religion.

12

Interim Conclusion: The State of Play

The year 1700 marks a convenient rest stop in which we can take stock of the distances traveled since 1600 and before. With Locke, Boyle and Newton, modern philosophy has reached a new level of maturity compared to the pioneering works of Galileo, Bacon and Descartes. It may help to review the publication dates of some of the main works of the early period.

Galileo	*The Sidereal Messenger*	1610
Bacon	*Novum Organan*	1620
Descartes	*Meditations*	1641
Hobbes	*Leviathan*	1651
Spinoza	*Ethics*	1677
Newton	*Principia*	1687
Locke	*Essay*	1690

All these thinkers aim to overturn the scholastic tradition of the Catholic Church and to develop a scientific conception of knowledge. This is clearly the main unifying theme. At the same time, most of the philosophers are deeply concerned about the ethical and religious implications of this upheaval. In this Descartes' *Meditations* is central. Although the later works of the other philosophers can be seen largely as reactions to his thought, they retain his religious concerns and, like Descartes, they try to answer them by rethinking the nature of metaphysics and epistemology.

Interim Conclusion: The State of Play

We can see a clear line of progression from Bacon to Descartes. Bacon calls for a unified science and a new philosophy, and Descartes unwittingly provides it. We can also see a line of development from Descartes to Hobbes, Newton and Locke. Hobbes thinks that Descartes' dualistic metaphysics is incompatible with his mechanistic view of science and argues for materialism. Locke thinks that his epistemology relies too much on rationalism and innate ideas. Newton's physics replaces Descartes' inadequate conceptions of motion and force.

However, this picture leaves out Spinoza, whose work constitutes a different line of development from the above. Towards the end of his life, Descartes began to rethink his earlier Bacon-like view of the nature of human progress. It does not consist in the scientific mastery over nature, but rather the control over our own passions. This line of thought leads to Spinoza's ethics.

Some Patterns

Reviewing these developments, we are struck by six characteristics.

1) First, philosophy has become increasingly secularized. Although Locke argues for the existence of God and defends a reasonable Christianity, God does not have a central role in his metaphysics, epistemology, and politics. Indeed, one might wonder whether the very idea of the divine is compatible with Locke's empiricist theory of ideas, despite his claims to the contrary. Although Newton also argues for the existence of God, his physics lends itself to the following interpretation: after having created the universe, God has no role in its working thereafter, which is purely mechanical. The universe is like a machine that functions independently of divine intervention. In this respect, we might compare Locke and Newton to Descartes, for whom God has a more central epistemological importance. The contrast is all the more great compared to the earlier scholastic thinkers. However, this does not mean that Scholasticism is dead by 1700. During the time of Locke, universities still taught scholastic thought, but the innovative thinking of the time takes place outside of the traditional universities and addresses quite different issues. Indeed, none of the philosophers that we have examined produced their major works within a university.

Furthermore, in contrast to Scholasticism, appeals to authority have little argumentative power in the early modern philosophers. Descartes' skepticism, Bacon's induction, Hobbes' materialism, and Locke's rejection of innate ideas reveal the redundancy of argumentation based on authority.

In short, there is a widening chasm between faith and reason, and religion and science. The major attempts to bridge that gap depend either on an unpalatable radical skepticism (as in the case of Descartes and Berkeley) or on an unorthodox reinterpretation of religion (as in the case of Spinoza). This point will lead to Hume's skepticism and to Kant's reply to him, which constitutes a new moral interpretation of the divine.

2) Second, the attitude towards the philosophers of ancient Greece has radically changed in comparison with that of the Renaissance. The ancient thinkers are no longer held in awe and are no longer an essential source of inspiration. In both Plato and Aristotle, the rational order of the universe was a sign of divine intelligence. Furthermore, human reason was able to grasp this order precisely because it too was divine logos, a part of God in man. Early modern thinkers and scientists, such as Copernicus and Descartes, largely shared this ancient vision. Compare this idea with Locke's later notion of nominal essences. Furthermore, ancient thinking was now viewed as outdated and based on scientific ignorance. Modern philosophy is now a young adult, which no longer needs its parents, Scholasticism and ancient thought.

However, this point leaves modern thought with an as yet barely perceived problem: Why is the universe rationally ordered and why are we able to describe that order so precisely with mathematics? In other words, to use Galileo's phrase, why is the universe written in the language of mathematics? Whereas Plato and the ancients had some answer to this question, mechanical philosophy apparently does not. Ironically, modern science cannot explain the mathematics on which it so heavily relies. This problem will lead to Kant's metaphysics of transcendental idealism.

3) Third, there is the absolutely fundamental problem of whether and how the principles of mechanistic scientific explanation apply to humans. If nature consists of solely the motion of inert atoms according to mechanical laws, and if humans are a part of nature, then humans too are mechanical and inert atoms. However, if that is true, how do we account for our self-consciousness, reason and will? In very different ways, this question exercised the minds of all the modern philosophers. In this respect, contrast Descartes and Hobbes. Descartes' dualism effectively denies that human souls are a part of the natural order. Hobbes, on the other hand, accepts materialism, a merely calculating view of reason, and denies the will. Locke tries to find an uneasy middle path between the two. Spinoza and, as we shall see, Berkeley advance dramatic, but very different, metaphysical solutions to this

problem. In retrospect, none of these theories appear compelling. Consequently, this problem also haunts the works of the later modern philosophers, Leibniz, Hume and Kant. And, despite their work, this fundamental problem continues, in a very different form, into the 21st century.

4) Fourth, we can see an emerging division between Rationalism and Empiricism. Rationalist thinkers, such as Spinoza, employ the Principle of Sufficient Reason as the basis of their thought. Everything must have a sufficient reason why it is so and not otherwise and, consequently, reasoning and deduction can show us a priori how the universe is governed. As a result of this, Rationalists tend to regard sense perception as an inferior source of knowledge. Not only is it subject to illusions but, more importantly, it fails to inform us why things happen. Because Rationalists think that in principle all truths can be demonstrated a priori by God, they also accept a form of determinism.

On the other hand, Empiricists, such as Locke and Berkeley, tend to regard all concepts and knowledge as derived from sense experience. Reason alone cannot give us information about the world. Hume, whom we shall consider later, argues that reason can only explicate concepts and that it can only yield uninformative analytic truths, such as 'all brothers are male.' Furthermore, the traditional Empiricists of the modern period claim that we can only perceive our own ideas. As a consequence, they face the problem of how knowledge of the world beyond those ideas is possible.

This distinction between Rationalist and Empiricist has to be handled carefully. First, modern philosophers did in no way consider themselves as belonging to a particular school of thought. 'Rationalism' and 'Empiricism' are classificatory concepts developed after the fact by Kant. Second, the distinction is simplistic. For example, we find many Rationalist strands in Locke's thought, and Descartes, who is considered a Rationalist, argues for the thesis that we can only perceive our own ideas, an Empiricist claim. Thirdly, Hobbes seems to be both. He has a Rationalist view of scientific knowledge and an Empiricist theory of concept acquisition.

Although the distinction is fuzzy and simplistic, nevertheless it does isolate two important general strands in early modern philosophy. In fact, the division became even more marked after 1700. Hume seems more explicitly Empiricist than even Locke and Berkeley, and Leibniz is more overtly Rationalist than his predecessors. In this way, history builds up towards Kant's project of reconciliation between the two traditions.

5) Fifthly, this was a period of political turmoil, unleashed by the Reformation and by the replacing of the ideal of a unified European and Catholic Christendom by that of a Europe comprised of independent nation states. Given this, there was a need to rethink political theory. In the early modern period, thinkers began to substitute the earlier authoritarian view of ethics and politics with more rationally based theories. In other words, the principles of modern science should be applied to society, as Hobbes saw. However, Locke's more mature theory begins to rely on the notion of individual autonomy, which was an essentially revolutionary idea at the time but, also, not easily reconcilable with the metaphysics of modern science. This process will lead eventually to the Enlightenment and the French Revolution. The reliance on individual autonomy for understanding both politics and ethics finds full expression in the philosophy of Kant, who also tries to reconcile autonomy and causation.

6) In the early modern period we begin to see women participating a little more in philosophy, which is, however, still very male dominated. Descartes discussed philosophy with Princess Elizabeth of Bohemia (1618-1680) who, as we have seen, had a decisive influence on his later views. He also corresponded with Queen Christina of Sweden (1626-1689) and moved to Sweden to be her tutor. Locke worked with Lady Masham (1659-1708), who was his friend for over ten years and who published several works concerning ethics and religion. She also corresponded with Leibniz, whose work we shall consider in the next chapter. Leibniz discussed philosophy with the Duchess Sophie and her daughter, Sophie Charlotte. These discussions with Sophie Charlotte were especially important. She asked him to write down his comments to her queries, so that she could consider them at her leisure, and these notes later resulted in his *Theodicy*, the only large philosophical work that Leibniz published during his lifetime. Around 1690, the Countess Ann Conway (1631-79) wrote *The Principles of the Most Ancient and Modern Philosophy*, which influenced Leibniz.

Interim Conclusion: The State of Play

There were other women philosophers during the early modern period. The Duchess of Newcastle, Margaret Cavendish (1623-1673), wrote five philosophical works, including *Grounds of Natural Philosophy* (1668). In 1701, Catherine Cockburn (1679-1750) published her book, *Defence of Locke.* In short, there are initial signs of the greater intellectual freedom of upper class women during the modern period, which culminated in Mary Wollstonecraft's (1759-1797), *A Vindication of the Rights of Woman.*

13

Leibniz: New Questions

Gottfried Leibniz (1646–1716) was perhaps the most intelligent person of the 18th century. For example, he came as close as anyone could at that time to developing the computer without having electronic circuitry at his disposal. Independently of Newton, he invented the differential and integral calculus. He had an extraordinarily active life in many fields, and perhaps for this reason, his genius never quite achieved full expression. His life was laden with distractions. Overly optimistic, he started many ambitious projects, and he hated to leave a task unfinished.

A Busy Life

Leibniz was a precocious and self-confident young man, who completed his Ph.D. in law at the age of 20, after which he decided to work as legal advisor for the Elector of Mainz. For the rest of his life, he worked in the service of and as advisor to German nobility. He used these positions to advance many practical ideas. For example, as a young man, he worked on legal reform and he invented new systems of library cataloguing. Later, he advocated many ideas to aid the plight of the poor, such as councils of health and the publication of medical statistics to reduce the dangerous epidemics, as well as economic councils and surveys to improve manufacturing and agriculture. He recommended the setting up of a bureau of information and a department store. By the end of his life, he was a major European diplomat, employed by five European courts: Hanover, Brunswick, Berlin, Vienna and St. Petersburg.

A major turning point in his life came in 1672, when he was sent to Paris on a diplomatic mission. There, Leibniz made friends with the famous philosophers Arnauld and Malebranche, and the mathematician Huygens. Realizing the inadequacy of his knowledge of mathematics, he studied under the guidance of Huygens, and soon afterwards, he had developed the calculus. In 1673, he presented his calculating machine that could multiply and divide figures of 12 digits to the Royal Society of London. In October 1676, he returned to Germany via Holland and spent four days in discussions with Spinoza.

Leibniz had three life long fundamental projects. The first was to develop an alphabet of human thought, which would allow all reasoning to be represented in logical form. With this idea in mind, he invented his calculating machine. Furthermore, he developed the idea of binary numbers, and did pioneering work in formal logic, developing the first logical formal systems. He planned a system for giving all possible thoughts a number. Moreover, he realized that a computational theory of knowledge would require a huge database. In this spirit, he conceived an extensive, systematic encyclopedia of knowledge, and tried to establish academic societies in order to find collaborators to work on the encyclopedic project. For example, in 1700, he founded the Berlin Society of Sciences. Realizing that these academies would need money, he worked on income-generating projects, such as the draining of the Harz silver mines and the development of silk farms.

Leibniz's second project was to bridge the schism between the Catholic and Protestant churches. Following on from the ideas of earlier essays, in 1679, he offered to write a work that would serve as a theology for both Protestants and Catholics. Before embarking on this task, he tried to seek assurance from the Vatican that his interpretations of crucial theological points would not be considered heresy. The project was halted because of the death of his patron, Duke Friedrich. This proposal was in part motivated by the political turmoil of the time, which had its roots in religious divisions. Leibniz thought that these in turn were based on metaphysical misunderstandings, and therefore he sought to clarify theology.

His third life-long project was physics. Leibniz was unhappy with all the major modern schools of physics, including those of Descartes and Newton.

In a large part, Leibniz's mature metaphysics grew from these three projects. As he worked more deeply in each one of them, they pointed more and more towards common metaphysical conclusions. In this way Leibniz's metaphysics is a combination of his views on physics, language and theology.

Aims and Strategy

Leibniz's main metaphysical aim is to reject the materialism inherent in modern thought, especially in that of Newton. The basis of Leibniz's metaphysics is two simple propositions: the universe consists solely of substances and their properties, and these substances are dimensionless points of energy or force. This position immediately implies that our normal view that substances are things made of matter extended in space and time must be based on an illusion. In other words, Leibniz aims to replace a Newtonian ontology of material objects with one of dimensionless points of energy.

Leibniz has two arguments for these metaphysical assertions. Both are based, in different ways, on a fundamental and instructive rejection of aspects of Newton's physics. The publication in 1687 of Newton's *Principia* meant the gradual replacement of Cartesian physics by the more comprehensive Newtonian system. Leibniz, however, saw deep problems with Newton's physics.

1) The first argument

The first argument claims that space and time are not real. The argument is as follows:

1. Space and time are nothing but a system of relations.
2. All relations are ideal.
3. Therefore, space and time are ideal.

Given this argument, Leibniz can show that matter, which occupies space and time, is also ideal. Given these conclusions, he claims that a theory of motion requires the basic idea of energy or force. He argues that, given that space and time are unreal, a physical theory of motion requires the existence of irreducible forces.

2) The second argument

In the second argument, he claims that substance must be an indivisible simple or, in other words, that anything with parts cannot be a substance or an ultimate constituent of reality. From this, he concludes that reality consists of an infinity of dimensionless points.

Argument 1: Space and Time

For the sake of clarity, I shall split this argument into three stages. First, Leibniz argues against Newton's absolute theory of space and time and in favor of a relational view. Second, he contends that relations are only ideal. Third, he reasons that the physics of motion requires the existence of forces or energy.

1) Space and Time are Relations

In the last year of his life, 1716, Leibniz expounded his theory of space and time in his letters to Clarke. In these letters, he advocates a relational theory of space and time, directly opposed to the Newtonian absolute theory advanced by Clarke.

According to the Newtonian theory, space is logically prior to matter, which may or may not occupy it. Space is an unlimited whole and any region of space is a part of the one unlimited infinite whole. Bodies occupy parts of space and, although bodies have volume, space is not a property of bodies. Similar points apply to Newton's absolute conception of time.

In contrast, Leibniz's own theory of space and time denies the existence of absolute space and time. Space is not a container that exists logically prior to and independent of physical bodies. It is merely a system of relations. Leibniz affirms that the existence of matter is logically prior to the existence of space: physical objects or forces happen to be ordered spatially and space is nothing over and above these spatial relations. Leibniz claims to have decisive arguments against Newton's theory and in favor of his own.

1) First, he points out the different implications of Newton's and his own theories. The absolute theory entails that it is meaningful to suppose that a finite, material universe could have been differently situated in absolute, infinite space. For example, the collection of all material bodies could have been situated 10 meters to the left of where it actually is located. Its position could have been different in relation to absolute space. In contrast, Leibniz's relational theory implies that such a supposition is not meaningful. This view implies that it is senseless to suggest that all matter could have been created in a different position and can change position in space. There is no absolute space and an object can change position only relative to another object. Space is nothing over and above the spatial relations between objects and, consequently, it is meaningless to suppose that all objects could have been differently situated.

Next, Leibniz argues that the Principle of Sufficient Reason favors his own theory over that Newton's theory He says that God could have no possible reason for creating the universe in a different region of space or at a different period of time. Since everything must have a sufficient reason, it cannot make sense to say that the universe could have been created earlier or elsewhere in space; these cannot be genuine alternatives, contrary to the claims of the absolute theory. Therefore, the theory is false. The argument is as follows. 'P' stands for any statement about the position of all material things in relation to absolute space.

1. The absolute theory implies that P is meaningful.
2. The Principle of Sufficient Reason implies that P is meaningless.
3. <u>The Principle of Sufficient Reason is true</u>.
4. Therefore, the absolute theory is false

A similar argument applies to time. Newton's theory implies that the universe could have been created earlier or later than it in fact was with respect to absolute time. However, according to Leibniz's relational theory, these claims are meaningless, because time is nothing over and above the temporal relations between events. There is no absolute time. God creates time by creating temporally related events. There can be no time before the creation of events. Leibniz then argues that Newton's view contravenes the Principle of Sufficient Reason and, therefore, must be false.

2) Second, Leibniz challenges Newton's view on theological grounds. The Newtonian claim that space and time are absolute and infinite entities contradicts the uniqueness of God. If God is the only infinite individual, space and time cannot be absolute and infinite.

3) Third, Newton's theory is a violation of the Principle of the Identity of Indiscernibles, the claim that indiscernable things are identical. Points and empty regions of absolute space are clearly qualitatively similar in all respects (i.e. they are indiscernible). Yet the absolute theory maintains that they are numerically distinct.

2) Relations are Not Real

Leibniz's argument for this claim is based on his theory of language, according to which all propositions are reducible to those that have a subject-predicate form. A subject-predicate proposition has two parts. Consider the subject-predicate proposition 'Adam is ill.' The subject term of this proposition is 'Adam,' which refers to the individual Adam. The predicate term is 'is ill,' which attributes a property to Adam. A subject-predicate proposition is one that has the form 'S is P.' In contrast, a relational statement has the basic form 'aRb.' It asserts that the individual a stands in the relation R to the individual b. It has three parts.

Leibniz argues that all relational statements of the form 'aRb' can be reduced to propositions of the subject-predicate form 'S is P.' For example, the statement 'book A is heavier than book B' follows logically from the two subject-predicate propositions 'Book A has a weight of 2lbs' and 'Book B has a weight of 1 lb.' Given this kind of reduction, Leibniz argues that the universe can be completely described with subject-predicate propositions. The ontological counter part of this thesis about language is that only substances and their properties exist. In other words, relations are purely derivative.

When this thesis about relations is combined with Leibniz's relational theory of space and time, it implies that space and time are purely derivative. In this sense, space and time are not real. Consequently, neither are the material objects that appear to be extended in them. The fundamental nature of the physical universe must be something else.

3) The Need for Forces

Leibniz deduces what this 'something else' is through the nature of motion. According to Newton's theory, absolute motion is possible. It is motion with respect to absolute space for a period of absolute time. In contrast, Leibniz claims that there can be no such thing as motion against the background of unmoving absolute space.

However, according to Leibniz, motion cannot be purely relational because all relations must be reducible to the properties of some substance. In other words, a purely relational theory of motion is impossible. Consequently, there must be some factor other than absolute space and time to distinguish absolute and relative motion. Therefore, if motion is real, then it must be grounded in something apart from mere changes in relative position. This something else is force, which produces motion.

1. A purely relational theory of motion is impossible, because all relations are ideal.
2. Absolute motion with respect to absolute space and time is impossible, because there is no absolute space and time.
3. The only other possible ground for distinguishing absolute <u>and relative motion is force.</u>

4. Therefore, if motion exists then forces must exist.

To understand premise 1, consider the following. If A is moving relative to B, then B is moving relative to A. If all motion were relative, then that we could not affirm that the motion is a property of A, nor that it is a property of B. However, it must be property of something, because all relations are reducible. Therefore, there must be way to distinguish absolute and relative motion in order to be able to affirm whether it is A or B that is moving.

According to Leibniz, force is non-arbitrary. For example, if A and B are moving relative to each other, then at least one of the bodies must have been endowed with a positive force that caused the motion. In other words, active force allows us to affirm whether it is A or B that is moving absolutely. In summary, when we consider motion as merely the changing of relative position, it is utterly arbitrary whether A or B moves. However, there is more to motion than changes in position, because the reality of motion must be grounded in forces, which are absolute.

Argument 2: Infinite Divisibility

Leibniz's second argument is for the thesis that the universe consists of substances that are dimensionless points. It is based on the premise that a substance cannot have parts. It can be summarized as follows:

1. Substances do not depend for their reality on anything else.
2. Anything with parts depends for its reality on those parts.
3. Therefore, anything with parts cannot be a substance.

The conclusion of this argument is that all substances must be simples; they cannot have parts. Leibniz uses this conclusion to argue further that matter cannot be a substance and that all substances must be dimensionless points, which he calls monads.

Leibniz supports this argument by claiming that there cannot be any pure compounds or aggregates. A pure compound would be one without simple constituents. In other words, it would be infinitely divisible. Leibniz rejects the claim that something real can be infinitely divisible as absurd. He argues that there cannot be an infinite regress of dependency; such a regress must end somewhere. And if it must end, there must be indivisible simples. In which case, a compound is simply an aggregation of those simples.

Leibniz coins the phrase 'the labyrinth of the composition of the continuum' to refer to the problem of how things in the world can be composed out of a continuum. Anything in space is infinitely divisible because space does not consist of discrete units, but rather is a continuum. Atomists cannot explain how an indivisible atomic unit can exist in a continuum. Genuine atoms should be indivisible, but anything that exists in space is infinitely divisible. Atomism cannot solve the problem of the continuum but, at the same time, anything real cannot be infinitely divisible.

The above argument reveals the structure of Leibniz's reasoning but not its full power. To uncover the strength of the argument, we need to consider his objections to Newton's theory of gravity and to the idea of atoms. These objections are intimately related.

a) Gravity

One of the essential ideas of the mechanistic view of nature is that all changes in one physical body must be transmitted through some physical mechanism to another. However, Newton's theory of gravity violates this idea because, in his theory, gravity is a genuine action at a distance. In other words, according to Newton's theory of gravity, a body can affect immediately other distant bodies without any intervening mechanism. For this reason, Leibniz rejects Newton's notion of gravity, calling it a miraculous force.

As an alternative, in 1689, Leibniz published an article, *Essay Concerning the Causes of the Motions of the Heavenly Bodies*, in which he attempts to give an mathematically precise explanation of the movement of the planets which is thoroughly mechanistic, i.e. without relying on the apparently occult force of gravity. Leibniz's rejection of gravity also forms part of his argument against atomism, as we shall see now.

b) Atoms

Leibniz argues that atomism cannot explain cohesion, that is how a collection of atoms constitutes a single body. If only atoms exist, then the atomist cannot appeal to a distinct cohesive force to explain how atoms cohere. Furthermore, the idea of a cohesive force is essentially similar to that of gravity but on a microscopic scale. Therefore, atomism violates the basic principle of mechanistic science.

Some thinkers try to explain cohesion by claiming that atoms had something akin to hooks and eyes to hold them together. However, this merely repeats the problem. If atoms have different parts, then there must be some explanation of how the parts cohere together. Obviously, this kind of solution reproduces the problem ad infinitum. Furthermore, if atoms have different shapes, then they have distinguishable parts and they would not really be indivisible atoms. Leibniz rejects the very notion of a physical atom, because all matter is infinitely divisible.

Furthermore, a non-divisible atom would have to be a body of perfect hardness. Such bodies would have no flexibility. Consequently, in any collision they would instantly change direction. According to Leibniz, there can be no instantaneous reactions, because real collisions always take time. The bodies involved always have a size, and they are neither infinitely hard nor elastic. Consequently, it takes time for the first body to squash the second and for the first to slow down as the second accelerates. Such is the mechanism by which forces are transferred.

In summary, one of Leibniz's criticisms of Newton's physics is that Newton treats particles as if they were both infinitely hard and capable of transmitting force instantaneously. He also treats them as if they had a location at a point i.e. as if they had no size. In these ways, Newton connects particles by occult forces that operate at a distance. In short, Newton's physics is idealized, and could not be true of the real physical world. (Newton was aware of these problems but he saw these abstractions as necessary to describe reality mathematically).

Conclusion

The two rather long arguments presented in this chapter point to a single grand conclusion. First, space and time are unreal, and therefore, the objects that are extended in them cannot be real either. Nevertheless, true motion must be distinguished from relative motion, However, we cannot draw such a distinction by positing absolute space and time and can only do so by postulating an ontology of forces.

Second, a substance must be a true unit. This means that substances must be indivisible and, therefore, they cannot have spatial extension. Therefore, spatially extended matter cannot be a substance, and all substances must be dimensionless points. Given the first conclusion, these dimensionless point-like substances must be points of activity or energy.

However, these claims do not explain how material objects appear to exist. How could three-dimensional material things be built out of dimensionless points of force?

14

Leibniz: From Physics to Theology

Leibniz claims that the universe consist only of substances and their properties. These substances are simple monads, as he calls them, or dimensionless points of energy or force, as the arguments against Newton show. Having established that the universe consists of these monads, Leibniz must answer the question 'What other characteristics do monads have?' Leibniz answers this question in his *Monadology* (1710). His reply is very surprising and strange. To understand it, we need two ingredients: Leibniz's theory of the identity of substances and his reaction to Spinoza. Leibniz sees the force of Spinoza's premises, but rejects his conclusion that God is Nature.

First Feature: Related to Everything Else

As a young man fascinated by logic, Leibniz began to think about the nature of truth, and he arrived at the conclusion that a substance's identity must consist in all of its properties, including its relations to everything else. He arrived to this conclusion as follows. Consider an individual such as Adam. This individual must be identifiable and distinguishable in principle from all other possible individuals, including an infinite number of possible individuals very similar to Adam. Therefore, each individual substance can only be individuated by all of its properties. Leibniz concludes that each substance is individuated by its complete concept, which includes its relations to everything else in the universe.

Leibniz expresses this thesis by claiming that every monad must reflect the whole universe. Each individual substance stands in relation to all other substances (M, 56). The complete concept of a substance A must contain its relations to all other things at all times. Since relations are ideal, these relations are reducible to the properties of each substance. In this sense, any individual substance or monad expresses or mirrors the whole universe (M,56). To see how it does this, we turn to the second feature of monads.

Second Feature: Alive

Perhaps surprisingly, Leibniz accepts Spinoza's claim that everything is to some extent alive. He argues that there is no radical difference in kind between apparently inert matter and living beings, but only one of degree. Leibniz claims that 'Nature makes no leaps.' Furthermore, because substances must be simple, they cannot be extended in space and, therefore, monads are non-spatial. This reinforces the idea that they are non-material or mental substances.

Furthermore, there is one more essential point to consider. Although the universe consists of non-spatial monads, it *appears* to consist of objects in space and time and, thus, it must appear so to some minds. Thus, reality merely appears to consist of spatial physical objects. Reality is so perceived by the monads themselves that comprise reality. Spatial bodies are merely the appearances of and for mind-like monads.

In comparing monads to minds, Leibniz does not mean that all monads are self-conscious and have experiences and desires. In fact, he distinguishes between different kinds of monads with decreasing degrees of awareness: God, self-conscious minds, and non-conscious monads.

The monads that comprise what we regard as material objects are not conscious, but they have properties that are akin to perception and desire. First, nature consists of active forces. This means rejecting the conception of matter as something dead and inert. It implies that we should conceive of substance as having something akin to appetite or desire. It does not mean that all substances literally have desires, but rather that they have an 'internal principle' of change. Second, as we have seen, each substance expresses the whole universe. This does not mean that each substance literally has conscious perceptions of the universe. Leibniz affirms that an algebraic equation can express a circle, without resembling it. Nevertheless, it does mean that each substance has something analogous to perception.

Each monad reflects the universe from its own point of view, which is characterized by the relative confusion of its perceptions (M, 60). In a way, the perceptions of each monad are the same as those of any other because, in each case, these perceptions are simply a reflection of the whole universe. However, because of the principle of the identity of indiscernibles, no two monads can have the same perceptions. Consequently, the perceptions of monads differ with respect to their state of confusion. What each monad perceives more or less clearly defines its own unique point of view. This accounts for the illusion of spatial perspective. It explains how monads *appear* to stand in different spatial relations to each other when spatial relations are merely an appearance in the mind and when reality is non-spatial.

Third Feature: Self-Contained

Leibniz sees the logic of Spinoza's assertion that if there were more than one substance, then they could not be in causal interaction with each other (see Chapter 8). In fact, Leibniz reinforces Spinoza's assertion with his own arguments. Whereas, Spinoza employed this assertion to prove that only one substance exists, Leibniz rejects that conclusion and argues for the only remaining possibility, namely that each substance is like a world apart, independent of everything else. He rejects Spinoza's conclusion that there is only one substance on theological grounds. As we shall see, Leibniz argues that God wills the best of all possible worlds. Because of this, there must be as much variety in the world as possible and, because of this, there must be an infinity of substances rather than just one (M 57-58).

However, Leibniz accepts Spinoza's premise (i.e. if there were more than one substance, then they could not be in causal interaction) for much the same reasons that Spinoza does. The definition of substance as independent and the rationalist view of cause together imply that substances cannot interact. In a sense, a cause already contains its effects. Therefore, because a substance is independent, or a unity, it can never be the effect of something else.

To this, Leibniz adds a couple of his own arguments. First, substances cannot interact, because the proposition 'A acts on B' is relational and, as we have seen, all relational statements can be reduced to subject-predicate propositions. Thus, causation as a relation is only ideal. Secondly, each substance has its own complete concept, and this predetermines all its predicates at all times. Therefore, each monad develops in accordance with its predetermined nature, which unfolds without any outside influence, except that of God (M,11). In conclusion, like Spinoza, Leibniz denies the possibility of causal relations between substances. No created substance can interact with any other created substance (M, 7). In this sense, monads are 'windowless.'

Now, you are probably wondering how Leibniz reconciles this claim that there are in fact no causal relations between monads with his first claim that each monad mirrors the whole universe. On the one hand, each monad develops spontaneously and in isolation, in accordance with its predetermined nature. On the other hand, a change in any one monad is reflected in the changing state of any other monad, because every monad reflects every other monad. How can these two claims be reconciled? Leibniz's answer is that God determines the nature of each monad so that its state is coordinated in a pre-established harmony, without the need for any interference (M 51 and 78). In other words, Leibniz claims that his metaphysics shows the need for a divine pre-established harmony rather like Malebranche's (see Chapter 6).

Leibniz's conclusion is that the universe consists of an infinity of dimensionless monads that are alive, each one of which is self-contained, rather like Spinoza's Nature. This is what lies behind the appearance of a mechanical world of spatio-temporal objects. It is important to bear in mind that Leibniz advances his strange conclusions on the basis of apparently solid arguments and not as the result of speculation. Partly for this reason, Leibniz's philosophy became dominant in Germany after his death. This was despite the fact that Leibniz left no systematic exposition of his philosophy as a whole. The task of systematically reformulating Leibniz's philosophy was left to Christian von Wolff.

Theology

Leibniz is convinced that an all-perfect God exists. He offers several proofs of the existence of God, which we shall not consider here. Given this, we can explain Leibniz's view of creation as follows. There are an infinite number of possible worlds, the nature of each one of which is fixed logically by the complete concepts of the substances that form that world. In this way, the nature of each possible world is fixed logically. God chooses freely which of the possible worlds to make actual.

This separation between a perfect God and His creation has an important ethical implication, namely, that the world is imperfect. Leibniz is very aware of the problem of reconciling the existence of all-perfect God with the existence of evil in the world. This is the central theme of the *Theodicy*, 1710, which is the only philosophical book he published during his lifetime.

It seems that an all-perfect God would not create a world in which evil, such as unnecessary suffering, exists. Therefore, the existence of evil seems to be a refutation of the existence of a perfect God. Of course, Leibniz rejects such an argument. However, he also rejects those, such as Bayle, who claim that religious belief must be founded on faith alone, because belief in God contradicts reason. Leibniz tries to defend belief without abandoning reason.

To do this, he argues two points. First, the world is necessarily imperfect, because otherwise it would be identical to God who is all-perfect. Consequently, complaining that the world is imperfect is like affirming that it should not exist at all. Second, any way of improving this world would automatically make it worse. In other words, this is the best of all possible worlds.

Leibniz's claim that this is the best of all possible worlds seems patently false, and Voltaire satirizes it in his novel, *Candide*, published in 1759. However, Leibniz seeks to defend the claim, largely by explaining what he means. When he claims that this is the best of all possible worlds, Leibniz has in mind certain objective criteria of goodness. In particular, this is the most harmonious of all possible worlds, which means that the world contains the greatest diversity of phenomena and the simplest laws of nature. Each law allows that a 'maximum effect' is 'achieved with a minimum outlay.' Perhaps the best way to think about how Leibniz might have replied to Voltaire is as follows. It is certain that an all-perfect God exists and, necessarily, such a God would only create the best of all possible worlds.

Concerning Locke

In 1703, Leibniz began to write an extensive commentary on Locke's famous work the *Essay* (1690). By late 1704, Leibniz had his *New Essays Concerning Human Understanding* complete and ready for publication. However, when he received the news that Locke had died, Leibniz decided to not publish his work.

Leibniz's commentary on Locke takes the form of a dialogue between Philalèthe (lover of truth), representing Locke, and Théophile (lover of God), standing for Leibniz. It is instructive to compare the two philosophers by briefly examining Leibniz's work.

1) First, Leibniz takes issue with the very starting point of Locke's project: the rejection of innate ideas. Leibniz claims that there are necessary truths in metaphysics, ethics, logic, and mathematics, which are true independent of sense experience, and thus which can only be

known innately, or through a proof that is based on innate principles, such as those of non-contradiction and Sufficient Reason.

2) Another important difference between the two philosophers is that Locke assumes that we must be conscious of our own ideas. However, Leibniz has two ingenious arguments to show that there must be unconscious ideas. First, in deep sleep, we can be woken by a noise. Consequently, the noise impinges on our mind before we are even conscious of it. Second, if the majority of our ideas were not unconscious, we could not attend to those that are important. Our awareness would be crowded out. In fact, Leibniz claims that all our conscious ideas are composed of minute unconscious perceptions.

3) The debate regarding innate ideas has a deep metaphysical and theological significance for Leibniz. According to him, in denying innate ideas, Locke has rejected the basis of a proper understanding of religion. For instance, Locke's empiricist claim that all ideas are derived from experience makes the concept of infinity essentially problematic. Locke uses his theory of concept acquisition to argue that we do not have a positive conception of infinity. We only have the negative idea of a unit repeated without limit i.e. the concept of a potentially infinite quantity. This means that we cannot meaningfully talk about God's wisdom, power and goodness being infinite, for in such assertions the concept of infinity is being used positively and non-quantitatively. In contrast, Leibniz argues that such assertions can be meaningful, because the idea of infinity is not limited to what can be derived from a finite experience, since the idea of the infinite is innate.

4) In his *Essay,* Locke argues that there are no grounds for denying that matter might think. According to Locke, we can have no evidence against materialism. Leibniz wholeheartedly rejects this agnostic position. He argues that such a view leaves the immortality of the soul in doubt. The claim that the soul is immortal requires the assertion that it is not material.

5) Locke argues for an anti-essentialist thesis by distinguishing between real and nominal essences. Locke argues that we classify substances according to their nominal essence, and not their real essence, because the real essence of substance-kinds is unknown to us, In contrast, Leibniz thinks we classify according to real essences, even if they are unknown. He says 'the name 'gold' signifies not merely what the speaker knows of gold... but also what he does not know' (Remnant and Bennett, p. 354).

15

Berkeley: The Denial of Matter

George Berkeley (1685–1753) viewed Locke's philosophy as skeptical and atheistic. Berkeley overcomes these two faults with one dramatic stroke, by denying the existence of material substance. Minds and their ideas are all that exist. Our ideas of sense perception are not caused by material objects that lie behind a veil of perception, but directly by God. What we call objects are simply our ideas of sense, which exist only in the mind. Berkeley defends his strange views with apparently very persuasive arguments.

A Life of Conviction

Berkeley entered Trinity College, Dublin, when he was only fifteen. In 1707, he published a work on mathematics and was made a fellow at Trinity. He also took holy orders in the Anglican Church. That same year, 1707, Berkeley first conceived the bold idea that matter must be unreal. He began writing. His *Essay Towards a New Theory of Vision* appeared in 1709, and the following year he published A *Treatise Concerning the Principles of Human Knowledge.* Three years later, the *Three Dialogues Between Hylas and Philonous* were published. Berkeley was now only 28 years old, but these were to remain his best-known works. In 1713, he moved to London, where he made friends with the city's intellectuals, including Pope, and Swift. In

1721, he published *An Essay Towards Preventing the Ruin of Great Britain*. He began to plan and solicit support for a college in Bermuda. In 1728, he sailed for America with his new wife Anne, and purchased 100 acres of land near Newport, Rhode Island. At this time, Berkeley wrote *Alciphron*, a philosophical defense of Christianity. By 1732, the anticipated funds from England had not arrived, and Berkeley, disappointed, returned to London. In 1734, he was appointed Bishop of Cloyne and returned to Ireland to live in his diocese for 18 years. In 1744, he published *Siris*, which promoted the medical use of tar-water, made by boiling in water the tar from pine trees.

Looking over the life and writings of Berkeley, one is struck by one overwhelming point – that he was absolutely convinced that he had conclusively proved that matter does not exist. Did he?

The Fundamentals of His Philosophy

Berkeley's main philosophical aims are very clear. First, he denies the existence of material substance and second, he claims that the universe consists of only minds and their ideas, including God. He thinks that these philosophical views have great religious and moral significance, and we shall come to this point later.

Berkeley's argument for the non-existence of material substance is based on the thesis that we can perceive only our own ideas. We have seen that Descartes and Locke also argue for this thesis. Berkeley strengthens these arguments. Therefore, we can divide his argument against material substance into two parts:

1. We can perceive only our own ideas.
2. If we can perceive only our own ideas then matter does not exist

1) We Can Perceive Only Our Ideas

Berkeley's attempt to prove the supposition that we can perceive only our own ideas can be divided into three parts. First, he presents what has since been called the argument from illusion. Second, he shows that this argument undermines Locke's primary/secondary quality distinction. Third, he also attacks that distinction by undermining Locke's notion of abstract ideas.

1. The Argument from Illusion

Berkeley argues that we perceive nothing but certain sensible qualities, which are only ideas. He concludes that we only perceive ideas. To argue for this conclusion, Berkeley appeals to the so-called argument from illusion to show that sensible qualities are nothing but ideas and that we can perceive only our own ideas. This argument is the first step in Berkeley's attack on the existence of matter. The argument is as follows:

1. The real properties of an external object cannot change without the occurrence of a change in the object itself.
2. The colors I perceive can change without the occurrence of a change in the object itself.
3. Therefore, the colors I perceive are not the real properties of an external object.

The first premise establishes a criterion or standard that the real properties of an external object must meet. If those properties change, there must be a corresponding change in the object itself. The second premise informs us that the colors we perceive fail that test or criterion. For instance, perceived color can change if we wear colored glasses or if the surrounding lighting is altered. Since the colors I perceive are not the real properties of an external object, they are only ideas.

Next, Berkeley applies this argument to all the sensible qualities that we perceive. The sounds we hear, the tastes and smells we perceive, and the sensations of touch are all subject to illusion. This implies that all sensible qualities we perceive are only ideas or, in other words, that we only perceive our own ideas.

2. Primary and Secondary Qualities

One might try to resist this argument by appeal to Locke's distinction between primary and secondary qualities, by distinguishing between, for example, sounds as they are perceived, and sound as it is in itself, which is a vibration in the air. First, Berkeley replies that such a distinction leads to the absurd conclusions that real sounds (which are motions) can be felt or seen, but never heard, and that motions in the air can be sweet, loud, and soft. Second, Berkeley shows that the argument from illusion also applies to primary qualities. Perceived shape, size, speed of motion, and solidity all vary according to the conditions of perception, without requiring a change in the object, and therefore are simply ideas in the mind.

Third, Berkeley attacks Locke's claim that primary qualities resemble our ideas of sense, by contending that 'an idea can be like nothing but another idea.' We can compare two things only if it is possible to perceive them both. But, because we can perceive only our own ideas, it is impossible to compare an idea with a primary quality of an object, which cannot be perceived. It does not make sense to talk of resemblance when there is no possibility of comparison. In summary, Berkeley argues that the following three claims are inconsistent:

1. Primary qualities resemble their ideas.
2. We can only perceive our own ideas.
3. The claim that two things resemble each other requires that they can be compared.

Given that claims b and c are true, then claim a (the resemblance thesis) must be false.

Furthermore, Berkeley points out that all ideas are states of consciousness and that the primary qualities are supposed to be the properties of inert material substance. He argues that the properties of something inert cannot resemble conscious mental states.

3. Against Abstract Ideas

Berkeley has another way of undermining Locke's primary/secondary quality distinction. He says that the concept of the primary quality, such as extension, is an abstract idea, because the extension of an object is neither great nor small, since the terms 'great' and 'small' relate to the conditions of perception. Berkeley argues that there are no abstract ideas.

Locke claims that words become general by standing for general ideas, while ideas become general by abstraction. Against this, Berkeley argues that there can be no abstract ideas. For example, the general idea of a triangle would be of one that is not equilateral, isosceles, nor scalene. Berkeley points out that, since such a triangle is impossible, there can be no idea of such a triangle. He concludes that there can be no general abstract ideas. All ideas are particular. Berkeley argues that general abstract ideas are unnecessary. Words can be used meaningfully even when the speaker does not have an idea in mind when speaking. Particular ideas or images can be used to represent in a general way and, thus, general abstract ideas are unnecessary. In other words, all ideas are particular, but we may put these particular ideas to a general representative use.

2) Against Matter

Given that we can perceive only our own ideas, Berkeley presents us with a dilemma. Prior to philosophical reflection, most of us would assent to the following two claims:

1. Objects, such as tables and trees exist in the external world, and
2. They possess sensible or perceivable qualities, such as shape, size, and color.

The argument from illusion implies that these two assertions are inconsistent. If we insist that tables and trees are part of the external world, the argument shows that we never perceive them and their properties (because we perceive only our own ideas). If, on the other hand, we claim that we do perceive tables and trees, the argument from illusion shows that they are not part of the external world, because they must be merely ideas. In brief, either tables and chairs are only ideas or they are never perceived. Of these two alternatives, Berkeley argues for the first. It is contrary to common sense to assert that tables and all other sensible objects are never perceived, and he unhesitatingly draws the conclusion that they are merely ideas.

Houses, rivers, and mountains are all sensible objects and, by definition, sensible objects are what we perceive. However, the argument from illusion shows that we can only ever perceive our own ideas, which cannot exist unperceived. Therefore, sensible objects are only collections of ideas and cannot exist unperceived.

Berkeley answers the objection that we should distinguish between mediate and immediate perception. The objection is that, even if we can perceive immediately only our own ideas, it could still be argued that external objects are perceived mediately and that, on this basis, they can be distinguished from our ideas. This was Locke's and Descartes' position. In reply, Berkeley rejects the distinction arguing that the senses can only perceive what they perceive immediately because the senses cannot make any inferences. Once again, Berkeley forces us into a dilemma: either objects are immediately perceived, in which case they are ideas; or they are the unperceivable causes of our perceptions.

Material Substance

Having answered this objection, and having established that sensible objects are merely ideas, Berkeley turns to attack the notion of material substance. Berkeley's main argument against the existence of matter is a two-limbed argument based on the following two principles:

a) We can perceive only our own ideas
b) Matter is an inert substance that has certain sensible qualities

In the first limb, Berkeley argues that the notion of matter is contradictory given a) and b) above, because sensible qualities must be perceivable and hence must be ideas. No inert substance can have ideas; only minds can. The first limb of the argument is:

1. If sensible qualities are perceivable, then they must be ideas (by a) above).
2. No inert substance can have ideas.
3. Matter is an inert substance that has sensible qualities.
4. Therefore, the concept of matter is contradictory.

If one denies that sensible qualities are perceivable (i.e. premise 1 above), then Berkeley argues that the concept of matter is unknowable and meaningless. The second limb of his argument is as follows:

5. If sensible qualities are not perceivable, then they are essentially unknowable (because all knowledge must be derived from perception)
1. Something unknowable cannot be meaningfully talked about (because all words stand for ideas).
2. Matter is an inert substance that has sensible qualities.
3. Therefore, the concept of matter is meaningless

Since the notion of matter is either contradictory or meaningless, material substance cannot exist. In addition to the two-limbed argument, Berkeley makes other points against the notion of matter.

1) First, he argues that matter is a unnecessary hypothesis. In Part 1, section 18 of the *Principles*, Berkeley argues that material bodies are not necessary to explain our ideas. The existence of such bodies cannot be known either through the senses or reason. The senses inform us only of our ideas. Additionally, we cannot reason that unperceivable objects cause our ideas (since there is no necessary connection between such objects and our ideas). Since we cannot know whether external material bodies exist, it is not necessary to postulate them as the cause of our ideas. In section 19, Berkeley answers the objection that material objects are the simplest explanation of the ideas of perception. He replies that it is impossible to explain how inert matter could have any causal effect on immaterial minds or spirits. A similar point can be found in the philosophy of Spinoza.

2) Second, Berkeley attacks Locke's specific conception of material substance, which has two parts: sensible properties and a substratum that supports them. This notion of a substratum is incomprehensible. If substratum is supposed to support the mode extension, then substratum must in itself be extended, since the notion of a support presupposes extension. Consequently, every material substance that supports extension must itself have another type of

extension to give this support, and so on to infinity. Hence, the notion of an inert substratum is meaningless.

Conclusion and Summary

It is important to be able to appreciate the force of Berkeley's overall strategy. The conclusion of the argument from illusion is that we can perceive only our own ideas. From this starting point, Berkeley argues for one of the following two conclusions:

4. The idea of material substance involves a contradiction.
1. The idea of such a substance is really meaningless

The general form of Berkeley's arguments is that Locke, or any materialist, such as Hobbes, must assert either

a) External objects have sensible qualities or something resembling them, or
b) They do not.

If Locke chooses option a) then, Berkeley argues for alternative 1, on the grounds that it is a contradiction to suppose that an idea could exist in anything but a mind, and that the only thing that can resemble an idea is another idea.

On the other hand, if Locke chooses alternative b) then, Berkeley's strategy is to argue for option 2, based on the premise that something unperceivable cannot be known and because something unknowable cannot be significantly talked about.

Berkeley's remarkable conclusion presents the most fundamental challenge to common sense and to scientific metaphysics since Descartes' third stage of doubt. However, many of his contemporaries simply tried to ignore or sidestep this challenge. For instance, Lord Chesterfield wrote that Berkeley's 'arguments are, strictly speaking, unanswerable; but yet I am so far from being convinced by them.' However, Chesterfield's reply is contradictory for if Berkeley's arguments are unanswerable, then their conclusion is true. Likewise, Johnson kicked a stone and claimed to have refuted Berkeley. But this inadequate response simply ignores Berkeley's arguments. To face Berkeley's challenge fairly, as Kant did, we must answer two questions: Do Berkeley's arguments prove that we can perceive only our own ideas? Do they prove the conditional proposition 'Given that we can perceive only our ideas, then matter does not exist'?

Answers to Some Objections

Berkeley was well aware that his central claim would appear counter-intuitive to most of his readers and that he was swimming against the tide of philosophical opinion. Therefore, he tries to answer various objections to his idealism.

1) One objection is that Berkeley's idealism implies that there is no distinction between real things and illusions. He replies that he denies a philosophical conception of matter, not the existence of real things. Real things are simply ideas. There is a distinction between reality and illusion, although both exist in the mind. The distinction is based on the differences between the senses and imagination. First, ideas of sense are stronger and livelier; second, they have a coherence and order; third, they do not depend on our will. Since ideas of sense do not depend on our will, they must have some other cause.

2) If extension and shape exist only in the mind, does it not follow that the mind must be extended and shaped? Berkeley denies this. Extension and shape exist in the mind only as ideas, not as attributes of the mind itself. He points out that we see things at a distance in dreams, and that such objects exist only in the mind. More positively, he explains how we see distance. We do not directly see distance, which instead is suggested to us by features of our visual experience—for instance, by our ideas being blurred, out of focus, shades of color, and so on. Such features explain the apparent three-dimensionality of visual experience, despite the fact that we see our own ideas.

3) Berkeley argues that his views agree with common sense, which informs us that real things, such as chairs, are directly experienced. In contrast, the philosophy of Locke violates common sense, because it implies that real things exist hidden and unknown. By identifying the real with our ideas, Berkeley claims to make skepticism impossible and to defend common sense. However, Berkeley recognizes that his views run contrary to 'the prejudice of mankind.' He says that we should think with the learned and speak with the vulgar. In 1, 4 of the *Principles*, he claims that it is a popular opinion that houses and the like have an existence distinct from their being perceived, and he argues that this belief is contradictory.

Unperceived Objects

If sensible objects are only ideas, and if the essence of an idea is to be perceived, then surely objects cease to exist when I do perceive them. Is this true? Berkeley gives three different answers to this question.

1) First, he suggests that things can exist unperceived in the sense that I would have certain ideas under certain conditions. At *Principles* 1, 58, he claims that the earth moves, even though we do not perceive this movement, because if we were correctly placed we would perceive it. This view is phenomenalism: the claim that statements about objects are equivalent to hypothetical statements about sense experience.

2) Second, he claims that an object unperceived by me can be said to exist because it is perceived by other minds, particularly that of God.

3) Finally, Berkeley claims that unobserved objects exist in the sense that it is God's intention or will that, in the right circumstances, an observer would have certain ideas. Unperceived sensible objects continue to exist in the sense that God is ready to put certain ideas in our minds when we are in the right circumstances.

A Universe of God and Minds

So far we have examined only the negative part of Berkeley's metaphysics: his denial of material substance. However, in both the *Treatise Concerning the Principles of Human Knowledge* and the *Three Dialogues Between Hylas and Philonous,* he develops a positive vision of the nature of the universe: it consists of only minds and their ideas.

The Existence of God

Berkeley has two arguments for the existence of God. In the first, given at *Principles*, 29, he argues that the only possible cause of our ideas of sense is God. He does this in two steps. In the first, he contends that our ideas of sense must be caused by a mind by excluding the other options. Since they do not depend on our own will, ideas of sense must have an external cause. However, this external cause cannot be material objects. Furthermore, ideas of sense cannot be caused by other ideas, since ideas have no power of agency. Consequently, our ideas of sense must be caused by an external mind.

In the second step, he tries to establish that this mind is God. First, these ideas are always internally consistent, and this shows that they are caused by only one mind. Second, they are incredibly complex and varied, and this demonstrates the unimaginable power of the mind in question. Third, despite their complexity, these ideas are well ordered and this shows the benevolence of the mind. In conclusion, the mind that causes the ideas of sense must be unique, unimaginably powerful, and benevolent.

Berkeley argues that his God hypothesis is better than Locke's theory that ideas of sense are caused by material objects. First, the idea of matter is a contradiction. Second, according to Locke, God creates matter and matter causes ideas in us. Berkeley claims that his own explanation is simpler than Locke's: God directly creates ideas in our minds, without the need for matter. Third, matter cannot cause ideas because it is inert. By arguing that God directly causes our sensible ideas, Berkeley makes God the center of our lives and to destroy the atheism that he thinks is inherent in the materialism of Hobbes and Locke.

The Spirit or Mind

According to Berkeley, the only substances are spirits or minds. A spirit is a simple undivided active being. Insofar as a mind perceives ideas, it has understanding; insofar as it produces ideas, it is a will. Berkeley claims that we can have no idea of spirit, because all ideas are passive, and spirits or minds are essentially active. Nevertheless, we still know what the word 'spirit' means, because each of us is a spirit and is directly aware of his own being. Consequently, we do have the notion of a spirit. Berkeley says, 'My own mind and own ideas, I have immediate knowledge of.'

Conclusion

In some respects, Berkeley's metaphysics is similar to Leibniz's. Both deny the existence of matter and both argue that the universe consists of minds and their ideas. However, notice that they reach these idealistic conclusions in very different ways. Leibniz does so by rationally challenging the inconsistencies in Newtonian physics, such as its inability to handle the problem of the continuum. Berkeley does so by apparently taking Empiricist epistemological principles to their logical conclusion. Although some British intellectuals dismissed or tried to evade Berkeley's arguments, the Scottish philosopher Hume took them to heart.

16

Hume: Skepticism and Naturalism

With typical irreverence, Hume declares: 'If we take in our hand any volume of divinity or school metaphysics, for instance; let us ask, Does it contain any abstract reasoning concerning quantity and number? No. Does it contain any experimental reasoning concerning matter of fact and existence? No. Commit then to the flames: for it can contain nothing but sophistry and illusion.' This quotation captures the spirit of Hume's anti-metaphysical views and of his skeptical Empiricism.

Hume's Life

Like Descartes, David Hume (1711–1776) had a confused adolescence. At the age of 12, he entered Edinburgh University, and found that he had 'an insurmountable aversion to everything but the pursuits of philosophy and general learning,' Three years later, he left university without having graduated. By the time he was 17, he had lost all religious belief. In 1726, at the insistence of his family, he returned to university to study law, but once again left without a degree. In 1734, he went to France for three years where he completed the *Treatise on Human Nature,* published in 1739-40. Hume complained that his work 'fell dead-born from the press.' His readers complained that the work was too difficult.

In 1744, he was refused the Chair of Philosophy at Edinburgh because of his religious heterodoxy. He became secretary to Lieutenant-General St. Clair joining him on missions to Ireland, Vienna, and Turin. Meanwhile, he was trying to make his views more accessible and writing furiously. In 1748, he published *An Enquiry Concerning Human Understanding* and, in 1751, the *Enquiry Concerning the Principles of Morals*. His *Essays, Moral and Political* and *The Spirit of Laws* were published in 1748. In 1751, Hume completed the *Dialogues concerning the Principles of Natural Religion*, which were published only after his death. In 1752, he published *Political Discourses,* which was popular among the Tories for its conservative views.

In 1752, he was refused a professorship at the University of Glasgow. Between 1754 and 1762, Hume wrote the six volumes of his popular *History of England*, which established him as Britain's foremost historian. In 1750, he became Keeper of the law library in Edinburgh. Seven years later, he resigned from this post after being found guilty of ordering 'indecent Books and unworthy of a place in a learned library.' In 1762, Boswell called Hume 'the greatest writer in Britain.'

In 1763, he returned to France for three years. Hume was popular with French intellectual society, where the Enlightenment was beginning to emerge. Amongst his many friends in France were Diderot, D'Alembert, and Rousseau. Back in Scotland, Hume served as Undersecretary of State, from 1767 to 1769 and he became friends with Adam Smith.

The Basis of Hume's Philosophy

There are two general aspects to Hume's philosophy. First, he is an epistemological skeptic. Hume accepts the Empiricist principles inherent in the work of Locke and Berkeley and follows them to their logical conclusion: skepticism, specifically with regard to the notions of cause, objects, and self.

Second, he aims to provide a study of human nature by showing how certain beliefs arise naturally through the non-rational side of our nature. Hume substitutes a naturalistic explanation for rational justification. In this way, he aims to replace Rationalism with naturalism. He repudiates Rationalism in three ways. First, he claims that all investigation must be based on observation and introspection, rather than reason. Second, he challenges the traditional definition of a person as a rational animal, by emphasizing our feelings and passions. Third, Hume supports this emphasis on the feeling side of our nature with his arguments for skepticism. Typically, he gives a naturalistic and non-rationalistic account of the origins of certain beliefs after he has argued philosophically that these beliefs cannot be justified by appeal either to reason or to sense experience.

The best way to understand Hume's philosophy is in terms of two steps. The first consists of Hume's attempt to develop two epistemological principles that form the basis of his analysis. The second consists in the application of those principles to three concepts: causation, material bodies and the self. In each case, the outcome of these analyses is a skeptical argument that our fundamental ideas cannot be justified and the replacement of justification with naturalistic explanation

The Two Principles

The basis of Hume's philosophy consists in two principles. The first is the thesis that all ideas are derived from simple sense impressions, a claim that is similar to Locke's Empiricism. The second, which is often called Hume's fork, consists in the thesis that all judgments are either of relations of ideas and of matters of fact. Together these principles form a fundamental rejection of the Rationalism of Descartes, Spinoza and Leibniz. However, they have more radical skeptical implications regarding the nature of our fundamental beliefs, as we shall see.

1. Ideas and Impressions

In section II of the *Enquiry,* Hume divides perceptions into two kinds: impressions and ideas. All sensations, passions, and emotions are impressions; but to think of something is to form an idea of it. Ideas are faint copies of vivid impressions.

All perceptions are simple or complex. Simple perceptions cannot be subdivided while complex ones can. For instance, the impression of an apple may be divided into separate tastes, colors and smells, and is complex. All simple impressions come from sense or reflection. The latter, which includes desire, hope and belief, arises from reflecting on previous sense impressions. Hence, the impressions of reflection depend on those of sense.

Furthermore, every simple idea is a faint copy of a simple impression. For example, a blind person, who has no impression of color, cannot have any ideas of colors. All complex perceptions are made up of simple ones and all simple ideas are derived from simple impressions. Therefore, all perceptions result from, or are, simple impressions.

This result is important for understanding the limitations of the mind and is the basis for Hume's skepticism. In the *Enquiry*, he says 'when we entertain any suspicion that a philosophical term is employed without any meaning, we need to inquire from what impression is that supposed idea derived?' All meaningful words must stand for ideas.

In section III of the *Enquiry,* Hume claims that ideas and impressions do not occur haphazardly. They are bound together and united by association, which he compares to the force of gravity. Association works through three types of relations between our perceptions: resemblance; contiguity in time and place; and cause and effect. Because of these three relations, the mind passes naturally from one idea to another. Association connects our ideas and explains how all our beliefs and ideas are formed naturally.

Hume distinguishes between having an idea and actually assenting to or believing it. We can join the idea of a man's head with that of the body of a horse, without believing that such an animal actually exists. The difference between believing and imagining consists 'in their feeling to the mind.' The ideas of belief are more vivid, forcible, and steady.

2. Judgments of Facts and Ideas

In section IV of the *Enquiry,* Hume divides all judgments into two exclusive and exhaustive groups: relations of ideas, and matters of fact. The first includes 'every affirmation which is either intuitively or demonstratively certain,' such as 'a father is a male.' Such truths are discoverable by reason alone because they tell us exclusively about the logical relations between our ideas and nothing about what actually exists. To deny such a truth is a contradiction. In contrast, judgments of matters of fact are not demonstratively certain, because their denial is not a contradiction and their truth depends on what exists in the world. This distinction became known as 'Hume's fork.' It denies the Rationalist assumption that reasoning is sufficient for knowledge of the world because reasoning alone cannot yield knowledge of matters of fact. This point is an important for the development of his philosophy.

Their Application

Hume applies this theory of the origin of ideas and his fork to our fundamental beliefs about causation, external objects and the self. He argues that such beliefs cannot be justified.

1. The Causal Relation

Hume attacks the Rationalist conception of a cause, which has two aspects. First, the Rationalists thought that the effect was necessary given the cause. Given a complete specification of its cause, logically the effect has to happen. For example, consider the determinism inherent in Spinoza's philosophy. The second aspect of the Rationalist view of cause is the principle of sufficient reason that everything must have a sufficient cause why it is so and not otherwise. This principle is employed explicitly by Leibniz, but it is also present in the philosophies of Spinoza and Descartes.

Hume's skeptical attack is based on his fork, according to which all judgments either are of fact or of relations between ideas. In contemporary terminology, all meaningful sentences are either empirical (based on sense observation) or analytic (based on definitions). Hume's fork apparently shows that the justification of any judgment must be based either on reasoning from definitions, or on sense impressions. Hume's attack on causation consists in applying this fork at three levels.

1) The first is the scope of the causal relation. Hume argues that the claim 'all events have a cause' cannot be justified. It cannot be justified empirically, by observation, because no one can observe all events. Neither can it be justified by reason, because it is not an analytic truth. 'All events have a cause' should not be confused with 'all effects have a cause.' The latter is a priori because it is analytic. The former is not. The ideas of an event and a cause are distinct and thus we can conceive of an event that has no cause. Consequently, the idea of an uncaused event is not a logical contradiction, and Hume concludes that the Rationalist Principle of Sufficient Reason cannot be justified.

2) The second level is the nature of the causal relation. We assume that causation requires the idea of a necessary connection between events. Hume thinks that this idea of a necessary connection is without justification. In section VII, part II of the *Enquiry*, he says: 'the necessary conclusion seems to be that we have no idea of connection and power at all, and that these words are absolutely without meaning.' It cannot be justified empirically because there is no sense impression of such a necessary connection. All we ever perceive are events following one after the other. We do not perceive any connection between them. Therefore, the idea cannot be justified by appeal to sense impressions. The idea cannot be justified by reason either. Any two events are logically separate. There are no logical relations between them. If one event A causes another event B, the two events

are logically distinct, and there is no logical necessity that B should follow A. For example, it is not logically necessary that a stone thrown into the air should fall to the ground. Hume thus denies the Rationalist claim that we can have a priori knowledge of particular effects.

3) Third, Hume asserts that we apparently acquire beliefs about the unobserved future by reasoning inductively using the causal relation. We see that in the past A has always been followed by B, and conclude the next A will also be followed by B. Hume argues for a skeptical position about such reasoning; inductive reasoning can never be justified. First, it cannot be justified deductively. There is no contradiction in supposing that snow might taste salty in the future. He says that what does not involve a contradiction cannot be proved false by reasoning a priori. Just because the sun has risen every day up to now does not logically imply that it will rise tomorrow. Second, inductive reasoning cannot be justified empirically, by appeal to past and present observations. Hume argues for this conclusion by showing that inductive reasoning presupposes that nature will continue in the same way in the future. It assumes that nature is uniform. A causal inference from the observed present and past to the future requires the assumption that the course of nature continues uniformly, as it has done in the past. However, this assumption itself cannot be justified empirically by induction. We cannot assert that, because nature has been consistently uniform in the past, it will continue to be uniform in the future. This would simply beg the question. Furthermore, the assumption that nature is uniform is not an analytic truth, and so it cannot be justified deductively.

Hume's general aim is to replace rationalist justifications with naturalistic explanations. Thus, Hume explains the idea of cause in terms of feelings of expectation that arise from custom and habit. In section V of the *Enquiry* he says: 'all inferences from experience are effects of custom, not reasoning.' Because we are accustomed to certain conjunctions, we come to expect events to follow in a certain order. This expectation is spontaneous and natural, but it cannot be justified. Furthermore, the idea of causal necessity is derived from the feeling of inevitability that arises naturally when the mind is placed in certain conditions. The mind spreads or projects this feeling of necessity onto the events in external world. In reality, what we call cause is simply an observed constant conjunction between events

2. Material Bodies and Identity

In the *Treatise,* Hume examines our belief in the existence of external objects or bodies. Hume says that it is pointless to ask whether such bodies exist, because we cannot help but believe in their existence.

Instead, he seeks to explain the origin of this belief. To do this, Hume divides our belief in the existence of bodies into two parts. First, we believe that objects continue to exist when they are not perceived; thus, we believe that they have continued existence. Second, we believe that objects have a distinct existence, independent of the perceiver.

According to Hume, we are only ever aware of our own perceptions. Thus, Hume seeks to explain the natural and common belief that our impressions themselves have distinct and continued existence. He claims that these beliefs are not due to the senses or to reason, but to the imagination. First, he argues that such beliefs cannot be due to the senses. Obviously, the senses cannot be the source of our belief that objects continue to exist even when unperceived. Hume also argues that the senses cannot be the origin of our belief in the distinct existence of bodies because the senses present us with impressions only, and not with the idea that these impressions are distinct from our perceptions.

Second, he argues that the popular belief in the distinct and continued existence of bodies is not due to reason either. Inferences to this effect would have to be based on our impressions and such inferences require that there be an observed constant conjunction between our impressions and the objects. However, such a conjunction could never be observed, because we can only perceive impressions.

The common belief in the continuing and distinct existence of bodies has its origin in the imagination. The ordinary person attributes distinct and continuous existence to certain impressions, which are subsequently referred to as objects, when they exhibit constancy and coherence, which are features of series of impressions. A series of impressions has constancy when the impressions present themselves in the same order and do not change when interrupted. For example, when I look at a scene of mountains, and then turn away, they have not changed when I look back again. In this way, an invariable and uninterrupted series of momentary impressions is taken to be an identical object because of the natural dispositions of the imagination. We suppose that that the series of impressions continues in the same way, but unobserved, during the gaps when we are looking away. This explains our natural belief in the continuing and distinct existence of bodies.

3. *Personal Identity*

In Book 1, section V, part IV of the *Treatise*, Hume argues that the idea of a mental substance in which perceptions inhere is unintelligible. First, he points out that there is no impression from which such an idea can be derived. If the idea of a continuing self is derived directly from sense experience, there must be an impression of such a self. Hume notes that we are only directly aware of particular impressions, and that there is no impression of a self. All that we can find in introspection is a bundle of different perceptions in perpetual flux. Second, Hume argues that we cannot acquire knowledge of mental substance, nor indeed of any substance, from a priori reasoning. A priori reasoning can only inform us of the relations between our ideas; it cannot inform us of matters of fact.

Hume concludes that the idea of a mental substance cannot be justified by appealing either to the senses or to reason. Instead, we should explain the psychological origins of the ideas of the self and personal identity in terms of the workings of the imagination. Hume tries to explain how we naturally regard a series of perceptions as constituting a single mind. The imagination treats a series of momentary and distinct impressions as a single continuous self because of the resemblance between different perceptions and also because of causation. For example, when a series of perceptions seems to form a single causal chain, the imagination glides along the series, ignoring the differences between the perceptions, until it eventually regards the series as a single self, extended through time. However, there really are no necessary connections between these distinct perceptions. The idea of personal identity is a natural and inevitable fiction of the imagination.

Conclusion

We have seen how Hume argues for a skeptical Empiricism with regard to our fundamental beliefs about causes, objects and the self, which in turn he employs to argue for naturalism regarding those beliefs. As we shall now see, he extends those same arguments to ethics.

17

Hume: The Slave of the Passions

'Reason is, and ought always to be, the slave of the passions.' This sentence summarizes one of the main conclusions of both the *Treatise* and the *Enquiry Concerning the Principles of Morals,* whose aims are to apply Hume's experimental method to ethics. Hume hopes to discover the simple principles that describe human ethical life and, since ethics is based on the passions, he begins his moral philosophy with a psychological description of the passions. The quotation also summarizes Hume's rejection of a Platonic picture of the ethical life, which portrays the attaining of virtue in terms of reason obtaining knowledge of the good and control of the emotions.

The Passions

The passions arise from reflection on the simple impressions of pleasure and pain. The direct passions, such as desire, hope, joy and fear, arise immediately from pleasure and pain. For example, fear and hope arise when pain and pleasure are considered as uncertain. Examples of the direct passions include desire, joy, fear, hope and despair. In contrast, the indirect passions arise from a combination of impressions with other ideas. For instance, pride is a feeling of pleasure accompanied by the idea that one's own virtue, power or beauty is satisfactory. Love is a similar feeling accompanied by a similar idea about another person. Examples of the indirect passions include pride, humility, love, pity and generosity.

Hume distinguishes between the object and cause of a passion. For example, the object of humility and pride is the self, but their cause may be something quite different. For example, someone else's action may cause me to feel humility.

Hume calls passions 'modifications of existence.' They are merely felt, and they do not represent states of affairs and, consequently, they cannot be true or false, unlike propositions. This thesis is a basic premise of Hume's moral philosophy. From it, he derives the conclusion that passions themselves cannot be called reasonable or unreasonable, although they may be unreasonable in the derivative sense that they are caused by false beliefs.

Reason is Impotent

One of Hume's basic principles is that reasoning alone can never motivate an action. Reason is motivationally inert and, because of this, reason can never oppose a passion in the direction of the will, despite popular and philosophical talk of the conflict between reason and the passions. For example, both Descartes and Spinoza refer to the need for the rational soul to control the passions as if there were a conflict between them (see Chapters 5 and 8). According to Hume, this is a mistake because reason is motivationally impotent.

Hume derives this conclusion on the basis of what reason is. Reasoning is the process of deriving conclusions from premises or evidence. According to Hume, there are only two kinds of reasoning: deductions, which reveal the logical relations between ideas, and probable or inductive inferences, which concern probabilities about matters of fact. In brief, reasoning can only tell us what is true or likely to be true.

Hume gives three arguments that such rational considerations alone do not lead to action. First, he claims that, without a relevant desire or passion, we are entirely indifferent to what is true or false. Reason can appear to motivate actions because it draws our attention to facts that are relevant to our passions. For example, reason can remind us of the painful consequences of an action, but in such a case, what motivates us is the aversion to pain rather than reason itself. Furthermore, we are apt to confuse calm passions, such as the desire for the good and benevolence, with reason itself.

Second, reason can determine only what the relevant means are to some end. Our desires and passions alone determine what ends we have. To support this point, he argues that reasoning yields propositions that represent what is true or false and that such propositions are motivationally impotent because, unlike passions, they are not modifications of existence.

Third, Hume argues that one cannot derive logically a sentence about one ought to do from any combination of sentences about what is. His idea is that reason can only produce true or false sentences about what exists, and that, from such sentences, no claim about what ought to be done can be deduced.

Ethics

From the principle that beliefs alone cannot motivate action, Hume argues that moral distinctions are not based on reason but rather on feeling, thereby contradicting Locke's moral theory which compares ethics to mathematics (see Chapter 10). Hume's main argument is as follows.

1. Ethical judgments must be capable of motivating action.
2. Beliefs alone cannot motivate an action.
3. Therefore, ethical judgments cannot consist solely in beliefs.

Hume concludes, 'Morality, therefore, is more properly felt than judged of.' For example, virtue is defined by the fact it causes agreeable impressions of approval, and vice by the unpleasant impressions of disapproval. These moral feelings are characterized by a lack of personal interest. In summary, what we call moral judgments are really expressions of a certain kind of approval or disapproval, and they are not statements of fact at all. Of course, a person can make a empirical claim about what aspect of a situation causes him or her to have a certain moral feeling, but such a statement is a psychological statement and not a moral judgment at all.

Hume also argues that we can never give a rational justification for human ends in terms of rational principles. A person can justify his or her daily exercises in terms of the desire of health, and this desire can be justified in terms of the pain of illness, but a person cannot justify his or her dislike of pain. This, however, is an ultimate end that cannot be justified. A similar point applies to the desire for pleasure and to virtue insofar as it desired for its own sake.

To make the point vivid, he says, 'Tis not contrary to reason to prefer the destruction of the whole world to the scratching of my finger.' To understand this quotation, we need to recall Hume's definition of passions as real existences. As such, they are unlike beliefs, which purport to represent the world truly and which may be described as reasonable or unreasonable. Preferences and choices themselves are neither reasonable nor unreasonable.

Virtues and Vices

Virtues and vices are dispositions and states that are intrinsically agreeable or disagreeable. However, although virtue is desired for its own sake, Hume also stresses that the virtues are wanted as means to utility. For example, natural benevolence is universally praised for its general utility to society, but also because, like courtesy, it is immediately agreeable. In contrast to benevolence, which is a natural feeling for the interests of others, justice is an artificial virtue, which has its roots in self-interest. Justice is artificial because it arises from a social convention as a remedy for selfishness, which would otherwise impel people to appropriate the property of others. Justice is a necessary and socially useful invention. Hume's view of justice opposes theories that make justice a universal principle or a natural law based on reason, and those that make it depend on a social contract. According to Hume, contracts arise because of justice, rather than the other way around.

Natural Religion

Hume argues against a rationalist religious belief. He rejects the proofs of God's existence and the idea that miracles provide evidence for the Divine. Miracles could not be detected because we cannot rule out natural causes and, in any case, they cannot provide support for a supernatural power that lies outside experience. Hume substitutes rational justifications of religious belief with an account of its causes, which he traces in *The Natural History of Religion*. We project our hopes and fears onto the unknown causes of our fortunes, which we personify as rulers. In this way, polytheism arises, which changes to monotheism through the idea of a head ruler to whom all virtues are ascribed as a form of adulation.

Hume's *Dialogues Concerning Natural Religion* consist in a debate concerning the argument from design for the existence of God. Much of the dialogues are between Cleanthes, who represents deism, and Philo, who represents the skeptical atheism. Both agree that experience and reasoning are the sole sources of knowledge. However, Philo argues that our ideas extend no further than experience and that we have no experience of divine attributes. In contrast, Cleanthes presents the argument from design: nature shows signs of being designed and therefore, it is reasonable to infer the existence of a divine designer.

Philo gives four major objections to this argument. First, he claims that it is based on a false analogy because it assumes that the universe is a created artifact similar to a house. Second, only repeated experience can reveal the cause of a phenomenon, because cause is a constant conjunction. Since in the case of the universe as a whole such repeated experience is impossible, there is no reason to infer the existence of a designer. Third, Philo points out that Cleanthes assumes that instances of order do not have a natural cause. Furthermore, suppose that we assume that a divine mind has an ideal plan that causes the perceivable order of this world. Philo argues that this plan itself must have order, which also must be explained. Consequently, even granted the supposition that there is an ideal plan, the explanation would leave us in much the same situation as before. We are still left with a mystery. Fourth, Philo challenges the argument by claiming that the quantity of pain in human life warrants doubts about the goodness of any supposed divine mind.

Cleanthes' replies are directed mostly to the first and fourth objections. To the first, he contends that the nature impresses the mind immediately and irresistibly with the feeling that it is like a work of art. To the fourth, he replies that ultimate causes are unknown and that he is content to stop his enquiry with the mind of a Deity. To these suggestions, Philo claims that, at most, the argument from design shows us that the universe is like the body of an organism that naturally has a certain kind of organization. The idea of a pure spiritual substance is contrary to experience. The argument from design assumes that there has to be some inherent principle of order, and that there is nothing in the argument to suggest that this principle is not inherent in nature rather than pure spirit.

Conclusions

Hume's Europe of 1760 was very different from that of 1600. Hume was a close friend to the philosopher and economist Adam Smith, who developed his theory of international trade by watching the specialization of labor in a pin factory in Scotland. This was the dawn of the Industrial Revolution. It was also the beginning of the Enlightenment and, during his several visits to France, Hume became friends with several French Enlightenment thinkers. Additionally, Scotland produced many thinkers during this period and Hume has been called the philosopher of the Scottish Enlightenment. Other Scottish philosophers of the period include Francis Hutcheson (1694-1746), Adam Smith (1723-90), Thomas Reid (1710-96) and James Beattie (1735-1802).

In conclusion, Hume's philosophy is a form of both skeptical empiricism and naturalism that attempts to replace rationalist justifications of beliefs with their naturalistic explanation. His thought has had three major influences on European thought. First, his naturalism has had an important impact on later pragmatism and romanticism. The romantics drew inspiration from Hume's emphasis on feeling, as opposed to reason, as a source of our beliefs (see Chapter 22). The later pragmatists adopted Hume's idea that our beliefs can be given a naturalistic explanation rather than a rational justification. Second, many 20th century empiricist philosophers, such as the logical positivists, have found illumination in his form of skeptical Empiricism and, more specifically, his ethical theory has inspired recent non-cognitivist moral theories. Third, Hume's philosophy had a profound impact on Kant, who was awoken from his 'dogmatic slumbers' after reading Hume and thereby stimulated to try to consolidate modern philosophy into a grand synthesis.

18

Interim Conclusion: The Need for Synthesis

Phase two of modern philosophy is now over. Let us take stock and review the major conclusions and themes of this period, which covers roughly 1700 to 1750. Among the major philosophical works, there are:

Leibniz	*Monadology*	1710
Berkeley	*The Principles of Human Knowledge*	1710
Hume	*Treatise on Human Nature*	1740

We immediately notice two striking facts in comparison with the earlier phase of modern philosophy. First, there is a more noticeable divide between the Rationalists and Empiricists. Second, the conclusions of the major philosophers of this period are at the same time both more logical, and more contrary to common sense. Of course, their being against common sense in itself does not mean that they are false, and not all philosophers of the period argued for counter-intuitive conclusions; for example, the work of Thomas Reid, can be regarded as a defense of common sense against Hume's skepticism.

1. Rationalism and Empiricism

As we noted in Chapter 11, Rationalism and Empiricism are not schools of philosophy. They are labels that indicate some broad similarities and differences between two groups of philosophers. Nevertheless, these labels have more significance in this later phase of modern philosophy.

Empiricism of the modern period is marked by two fundamental claims: the thesis that we can perceive only our own ideas and the assertion that all concepts are derived from sense-experience. Sense-experience is the ultimate source of knowledge and meaning and, therefore, reason does not yield new knowledge but makes deductions from what is already known. The two central claims of Empiricism imply skepticism as Berkeley and Hume saw.

Rationalism in the modern period is based on the principle of Sufficient Reason. Nothing happens without an adequate cause and a complete specification of a cause logically entails the effect. This principle has two implications. First, it means that in principle all truths can be grasped a priori by reason and, as a result, reason is a superior source of knowledge than sense experience, which is subject to illusions and which never gives us knowledge of causes. Second, it implies that fundamentally all truths are necessary and this seems to imply determinism.

The contrast between Rationalism and Empiricism is strikingly vivid in the difference between Leibniz and Hume. It is as if at the end of the second stage of modern philosophy, these two thinkers have taken Rationalism and Empiricism to their logical conclusions. This indicates the need for a new start, which is provided in the third phase of the modern period by Kant's grand synthesis.

2. Contrary to Common Sense, but Logical

Earlier we noted how the views of the later modern philosophers were both more logical and contrary to common sense compared to those of their predecessors. This point does not repudiate or endorse any particular view. Sometimes, truth is counter-intuitive.

The views of the philosophers of this second phase are more logical in the sense that that their conclusions appear to follow validly from their starting premises. For example, it is difficult to find holes or errors in Berkeley's arguments for idealism. Similarly, Leibniz's arguments appear to be well grounded. Likewise, Hume's skepticism seems difficult to refute given his two epistemological principles.

At the same time, the conclusions of all three philosophers are in different ways an assault on common sense. In contrast, the views of

Bacon, Descartes. Hobbes, and Locke seem to accord more with common sense. Even Spinoza's metaphysics appears more palatable than Leibniz's. Consider Hume's reactions to his own views. He himself expresses incredulity at his own skeptical conclusions,

This combination of being both more logical and counter-intuitive has two interesting implications. First, it is a sign of greater confidence and maturity. It requires more self-assurance to argue boldly for a plainly counter-intuitive conclusion and, furthermore, to be at all plausible, it requires better argumentation. Since 1600, philosophy has become more self-confident.

The second implication is that the better or tighter the arguments appear, the more any attempt to deny the relevant conclusions requires a critical examination of the original premises. When counter-intuitive results appear to follow logically from a set of assumptions, then we must begin to challenge those initial assumptions, even if, at first glance, they may look innocuous. This is exactly what happened. Kant went back to the drawing board and examined the starting assumptions of both Rationalism and Empiricism and, as a consequence, philosophy took a new leap forward.

The above two points are linked to each other and to a third point. Both Rationalism and Empiricism have unfinished business on their plates. On the one hand, Rationalism has to explain why the world is rationally ordered, and why reason is able to grasp this order. As we noted in our review of the early phase of modern philosophy in Chapter 11, mechanistic science does not explain how we are able to describe that order so precisely with mathematics. Ironically, modern science cannot explain the mathematics on which it so heavily relies.

On the other hand, Empiricism confronts the problem of how knowledge of the external world is possible, given the assumption that we can perceive only our own ideas. How can I know that my ideas represent the world truly? Of course, Berkeley uses this kind of point to try to argue against material substance. However, he faces exactly the same problem regarding other minds, though he hardly realizes it. If Berkeley can only perceive his own ideas, how does he know that the universe contains other minds similar to his? The ghost of Descartes' doubt has not been exorcised.

Once again, Kant appreciated the force of these points, which seem to indicate the need for a radical rethinking. By undertaking such an evaluation, Kant tries to reply to the questions that Empiricism and Rationalism have left unanswered.

Some other Points

1) Scholasticism is no longer an important intellectual threat. Philosophers of the earlier phase of modern philosophy were pioneers struggling to establish the new science and combat the scholastic philosophy that dominated Europe at the time. This battle is now more or less over. Nevertheless, scholastic philosophy is still present in most European universities and, like their predecessors, the three later modern philosophers produced their major works outside of the universities.

2) The philosophers of this later period are beginning to contest aspects of the new science, rather than merely trying to develop it and argue in favor of it. For example, all three philosophers Leibniz, Berkeley, and Hume, challenge the notion of material substance, which was the darling of most of the early modern philosophers. All three also question the idea of mechanical causation. This does not mean that they reject modern science, but rather that they are willing to reinterpret its significance. With this point in mind, we can begin to see the slow separation of science and philosophy. All the early modern philosophers were experimental scientists. Even Bacon and Spinoza conducted experiments. During this early stage, science *was* natural philosophy. In contrast, despite the fact that Leibniz was an eminent mathematician and physicist, and despite the fact that both Berkeley and Hume had an excellent grasp of scientific principles, philosophy and science are beginning to separate.

3) Like their predecessors, religion is a central preoccupation of all three later modern philosophers. Religious concerns explicitly underlie the idealistic metaphysics of Berkeley and Leibniz, who regarded the views of Bacon, Hobbes and Locke as too secular. Taken in conjunction with point 1 above, this means that religion is less tied to Scholasticism than it was before. However, Hume's professed atheism and his attacks on the arguments for God's existence set a new tone for philosophy. As the Enlightenment unfolds, thinkers increasingly attack orthodox religion.

Furthermore, as this second phase of modern philosophy turns into the Enlightenment, politics and ethics become more important philosophical concerns. If Bacon was the last writer of the Renaissance, then Locke and Hume may be considered the first writers of the Enlightenment.

19

The French Enlightenment

The Enlightenment of the late 18th century grew, chiefly in France, from the attempt to extend the philosophical and scientific principles of the modern period to human social, political and moral life. It derives its inspiration from the earlier work of Bayle (see Chapter 6). More immediately, the Enlightenment thinkers were influenced by Locke, Newton and Hume in Britain, where freer thought was able to flourish more easily than in the absolute monarchy of France.

The Enlightenment is marked primarily by a belief in the ideals of progress, such as freedom from superstition, liberty of thought, social reform and material betterment, which fuelled an interest in history as an account of cultural progress. The Enlightenment is also characterized by a rejection of authority, especially that of the Church, and by an attempt to understand human values in non-metaphysical and non-theological terms.

These ideas inspired a generation of prolific French writers. For example, Montesquieu (1689-1755) studied different forms of government and legal systems and argued for political liberty, which requires the separation of legislative, judicial and executive powers. Condillac (1715-80) adapted the empiricist ideas of Locke to argue against the metaphysical systems of Spinoza and Leibniz. In his work, *Man, a Machine*, La Mettrie (1709-51) argued for a materialist view of the mind.

One of the great works of the period was the *Encyclopedia*, edited by Diderot and d'Alembert, the complete first edition of which consisted of 35 volumes, which appeared between 1751 and 1780. As well as functioning as a modern encyclopedia, the work contained social commentaries opposing the Church and the French establishment. However, the most eloquent and vociferous voice of the French Enlightenment was Voltaire, whose work we shall describe below.

The thought of Rousseau, on the other hand, begins to take us beyond the Enlightenment towards the Romanticism of the 19th century. Like Hume, Rousseau stresses the emotional aspect of human nature as against the rational and, unlike Voltaire, sees civilization as the source of human degeneration. His emphasis on the moral and political importance of human free will greatly influenced the later writings of the great German philosopher, Kant. Rousseau's political vision of the sovereignty of the people inspired the French Revolution.

In many ways, the work of Kant can be considered as culmination of the whole modern period. In the *Critique of Pure Reason* (1781), Kant identifies and diagnoses the conflicts between Rationalism and Empiricism, and produces a non-empiricist critique of Rationalism. By defining the limits of theoretical reason, he opens the way for a moral and political theory based on the freedom of the will. He defines 'enlightenment' as 'man's release from his self-imposed tutelage. Tutelage is man's inability to make use of his understanding without direction from another.'

By this time, the long dramatic battle, pioneered by Galileo, Descartes and Bacon, between modern science and medieval scholastic philosophy was over. Scholasticism was no longer an oppressive force. The Industrial age was beginning, and Kant's grand synthesis was itself to come under critical scrutiny.

Voltaire

Originally named François Marie Arouet, Voltaire (1694-1778) was a very famous and prolific man of letters, whose literary and philosophical works epitomized the spirit of the Enlightenment. He composed many successful plays, poems, several works in history and many essays. He was an astute businessman who became a millionaire, and he dabbled in science. As a young man, he visited England from 1726 to 1729, where he drew inspiration from the works of Locke and Newton as well as from the comparative liberty of English society. In 1738, he published the *Philosophy of Newton*, which was influential in replacing Descartes' physics with Newton's in France. After the great earthquake in Lisbon in 1755, Voltaire wrote his novel *Candide*, which, through the many misfortunes of the ever-optimistic Dr. Pangloss, satirizes Leibniz's claim that this is the best of all possible worlds. Voltaire's witty writings defend the ideal of political liberty and the doctrine of human rights, which should be respected by the state. They also advocate the idea of intellectual, scientific and economic progress.

Around 1751, after the suppression of the *Encyclopedia* (edited by Diderot and d'Alembert), Voltaire began to attack openly the Catholic Church and its doctrines. While exiled in Geneva, he published, in 1784, the popular *Dictionary of Philosophy,* in which he says: 'Almost everything that goes beyond the adoration of a Supreme Being, and submitting one's heart to his eternal orders, is superstition.' In 1778, the dying Voltaire returned from his exile to Paris, to great public acclaim. In 1783-90, Beaumarchais, the French play-writer, who also organized French military aid to the American War of Independence, financed the publication of the complete works of Voltaire in 70 volumes. Later, he also produced an edition of the works of Rousseau.

History

One feature of Enlightenment thought is a growing philosophical interest in history in part to provide evidence for the idea that humanity has progressed through the emancipation of reason. As a consequence, Enlightenment history tends to regard the medieval period unsympathetically. For this reason, the medieval period is referred to as the Middle Ages because it lies between the classical and modern eras. For example, Voltaire wrote a universal history of the period from Charlemagne to the Enlightenment with the aim of tracing the development of reason, culture, and industry. For Voltaire, history was really interesting only after the end of the 15th century. In his work on the philosophy of history, Voltaire noted that history should exclude supernatural explanations and myths and legends.

Condorcet (1743-98), who was an important political philosopher during the French revolution, also wrote a universal history in a similar spirit. He interpreted the past as a development towards a scientific culture, dividing history into nine periods; the ninth era begins with Descartes and terminates with the French revolution of 1789.

However, the German philosopher Herder, in *Ideas for the Philosophy of History* (1784), criticized this view of history as progress towards the Enlightenment. He pointed out that this approach prevents historians from understanding each culture and period in its own terms. Unlike Voltaire, and following Rousseau, Herder praised the medieval era as for its popular poetry, art and imagination. He also claimed that the development of the modern nation state was not due to the effects of reason, but rather other historical factors. Furthermore, he also criticized the tendency of Enlightenment thinkers to disparage earlier more 'primitive' forms of society as lacking in culture and happiness.

According to Herder, earlier cultures cannot be judged or understood in terms of 18th century ideals. With Herder, Rousseau and Romanticism (Chapter 22) the Enlightenment contained its own critique.

Rousseau

Jean-Jacques Rousseau (1712-1778) was born in Geneva; his mother died a week later. In his early youth, he wandered around Europe, almost destitute. In 1742, he moved to Paris, where he became friends with the young Diderot. In 1749, his essay, the *Discourse on the Arts and Science,* an attack on the corrupting effects of civilization, won a literary prize. Rousseau composed music and one of his operettas won acclaim. Tired of Paris, he returned to Geneva in 1754, and returned to the Protestant Church, having briefly been a Catholic. In his *Discourse on the Inequality among Men* (1755), he argues that humans are naturally good, and that injustice is caused by civil society. In 1755, Rousseau and his common law wife, Thérese, moved to a cottage on the edge of the forest of Montmorency, where he wrote his popular and romantic novel *La Nouvelle Héloïs* (1761). In 1762, he published two of his most well known books, the *Social Contract* and *Emile*, his work on education. These works made Rousseau an outcaste; his revolutionary works were banned and he faced imprisonment for heresy. Furthermore, his romantic naturalism and sensitive temperament brought him into conflict and quarrels with the philosophers of the time, most notably Voltaire and his old friend, Diderot. While Voltaire argued in favor of reason and progress, Rousseau praised spontaneous feeling and nature.

For a while, the naturalist philosopher David Hume befriended Rousseau. However, they quarreled and, in 1767, after a 16-month stay in England, Rousseau and Thérese returned to France, from which he was officially banned. His frank autobiography, the *Confessions*, was published posthumously in 1782 and, mainly because of it, he became the founder of the Romantic Movement, which flourished in the 19th century (see Chapter 22). His moral theory of freedom inspired Kant, while his doctrine of the sovereignty of the people fuelled the French Revolution.

Rousseau's political theory is best understood as a contrast between three conditions of life: a) the original state of nature, b) society as it ought to be according to the social contract, and c) society as it actually is. In their natural state, humans are different from the other animals not so much for their reasoning capacity, but rather for the soul's feeling of free will, which defies mechanical explanation. Humans are naturally free. They have self-love and natural compassion, but not egoism, There is no original sin. With this portrayal of human nature, Rousseau denies rationalism, mechanistic philosophy, Hobbes, and the teaching of the Church. For the sake of self-preservation, humans entered into a social contract but, in order for this act of association to be justifiable, it must not diminish our natural freedom. Consequently, the social contract must consist in the formation of a collective body, or general will, through which individual citizens share power. Through this contract, the social morality of justice, rights and duties replaces actions through instinct. Because of this, the individual citizen must be willing to follow the general will. However, the capacity to obey the law makes a person master of his or her own appetites and, thus, freedom finds full expression in a civil society governed by the social contract. He wrote: 'Obedience to a law which we prescribe to ourselves is liberty.'

In sharp contrast to both of these states, actual society corrupts natural human goodness and destroys freedom. Thus, Rousseau's famous opening sentence of the *Social Contract*, 'Man is born free and everywhere he is in chains' defines the problem of politics, the contrast between our fundamental nature and society as it actually is. The solution lies in the nature of the social contract, which describes how society should be.

The Revolution

As we saw in earlier chapters, Louis XIV was an absolute monarch. He justified his power in terms of the divine right of kings. The political thought of Locke and the English revolution of 1689 had a powerful influence on French intellectuals, as did the later American Revolution of 1776. When Louis XVI became the King in 1774, France was in debt and Louis was forced to impose hefty taxes on the middle and peasant classes. This led to a conflict between the National Assembly or parliament and the King, which in turn caused a popular and bloody uprising.

20

Kant: The Transcendental Turn

Kant's contemporaries praised him for the freedom and joyfulness of his soul. Apparently, his lectures were 'discourse at its most entertaining.' According to Herder, 'merriment, wit and humor were at his command.' This is not the impression we have of Kant from the *Critique of Pure Reason*. Kant himself wrote in his diary: 'The method of my discourse...appears scholastic and hence pettifogging and arid.' To comprehend this disparity, we must understand the background to the first Critique.

At the age of 31, Kant (1724–1804) became a university instructor, lecturing on a wide variety of subjects, including logic, geography, natural history, anthropology, mathematics, and physics. His first published works were mainly scientific. Kant's early philosophy was Rationalist, influenced by Leibniz and Wolff.

However, around 1770, after reading Hume, Kant awoke from his 'dogmatic slumbers,' and he went through a period of intense reflection for over ten years. Amazingly, Kant conceived his philosophy as a whole from the outset. In 1771, he was planning a project on the limits of sense and reason, which was to cover metaphysics, morals and aesthetics. In 1772, he hoped that the first volume would be ready in 3 months. However, as he worked through the details of his wide-ranging ideas, he became aware of the time and effort necessary to plan 'a whole new conceptual science.' In 1776, he wrote that his thought was blocked by a dam. So, finally, he decided to complete the work 'in the greatest haste within five months,' because otherwise, 'the work would probably have never been completed at all.' The first edition of the *Critique of Pure Reason* was published in 1781, when Kant was already 57. The second or B edition of the *Critique* appeared in 1787, which Kant rewrote in part because his readers had great difficulties in understanding his ideas.

Finally, when the dam broke, a huge torrent came pouring out. After 1781, he entered into a period of frenzied writing, articulating the implications of his theory for ethics, politics, history, religion, science, and art. His major works of this period are the *Groundwork of the Metaphysics of Morals,* 1785; the *Metaphysical Foundations Natural Science*, 1786; the *Critique of Practical Reason*, 1788; the *Critique of Judgment*, 1790; *Religion Within the Limits of Reason Alone,* 1793 and *The Metaphysics of Morals*, 1797.

The Basis of the First Critique

The portal into this startlingly vast domain of thought is the first major book, the *Critique of Pure Reason*. It is most important to understand Kant's aims in this work and, for the sake of simplicity, we can divide our exposition of them into three parts.

1. Synthetic A Priori Truths

The basis of Kant's theoretical philosophy is the notion of synthetic a priori truths. These are necessary truths that are not analytic. According to Kant, the two distinctions, analytic/synthetic and a priori/empirical must be separated. An analytic truth cannot be denied without contradiction, and any truth that is not analytic is synthetic. A priori truths are necessarily true, and a truth that is not a priori is empirical. Kant argues that not all a priori truths are analytic. These synthetic a priori truths are necessary truths that it would not be a contradiction to deny. Examples include 'every event must have a cause,' 'the three angles of a triangle equal 180 degrees,' and '7+5=12.' Such claims are necessary truths but, because they are not analytic, they can give us a priori knowledge of the world.

2. Their Importance for his Aims

According to Kant, such truths have an enormous philosophical significance. First, they form the basic principles of mathematics and science and, consequently, by explaining them, we can explain why the world has a mathematical and causal order. This explanation will amount to an argument against the epistemology of Empiricism. Second, the metaphysics of Rationalism effectively consists in a series of putative synthetic a priori claims and, as a consequence, by explaining how synthetic a priori truths are possible, Kant can show why such metaphysics is not possible.

Kant agrees that the idea of synthetic a priori truths is strange one and a major task of the *Critique* is to explain how they are possible. In so doing, Kant achieves his major aims. First, in explaining how such truths are possible, Kant shows why Empiricist epistemology is inadequate. Second, the conditions that make such truths possible is precisely what makes Rationalist metaphysics impossible. In summary, Kant develops a non-empiricist theory of knowledge to criticize Rationalist metaphysics.

3. How they are Possible

So, how are synthetic a priori truths about the world possible? Kant's answer has two elements that are the pillars of his theoretical philosophy.

a) First, he argues that experience has certain structural necessary conditions, which he calls the a priori forms of experience. Kant argues that space, time and the categories are the necessary conditions for any possible experience. Kant tries to demonstrate these necessary conditions with what are called transcendental arguments, the most important of which is the Transcendental Deduction. These arguments try to establish the structural features of experience, which any experience must have.

b) The second element is transcendental idealism. Kant argues that the world itself must conform to the a priori forms of experience. This involves giving up the assumption that the world is totally independent of the character of experience. Transcendental idealism is the claim that the world of spatio-temporal object is transcendentally ideal and empirically real. The world is empirically real because such objects are real in that they exist independently of us. The world is transcendentally ideal because such objects are, and must be, relative to the a priori forms of experience. In other words, although such objects are real, they are phenomena (relative to the a priori forms of experience) and are not noumena (or things as they are absolutely in themselves). Transcendental idealism implies that spatio-temporal objects necessarily conform to the a priori conditions of experience and, thereby, explains how synthetic a priori truths are possible.

c) Jointly these two elements or pillars of Kant's philosophy are necessary and sufficient to explain synthetic a priori truths. The two pillars jointly explain how synthetic a priori truths are possible, and how the sciences and mathematics work. The argument is simply:

1. Sentence 'S' states a necessary condition of experience
2. The world must conform to these necessary conditions.
3. Therefore, sentence 'S' is a priori true of the world

For 'S' we could put any synthetic a priori claim, such as 'all events are caused.' Premise one articulates a necessary condition of experience, which is the first pillar of Kant's explanation of the synthetic a priori. Premise two articulates transcendental idealism, the second pillar. Together, they explain 3. To repeat, Kant's point is that we can explain 3 only by 1 and 2 above. One of the main purposes of the first half of the *Critique* is to give support to the two premises and show how they explain synthetic priori truths.

To link this to Kant's aims, he argues that the fact that experience has a necessary or a priori structure (i.e. premise 1) refutes Empiricism, and that the world is transcendentally ideal (i.e. premise 2) shows that Rationalism is false.

Some Explanations

Since we have introduced many new concepts, it is worth giving some preliminary explanations of the main elements of Kant's philosophy before examining the details of the text.

1) Synthetic A priori Truths

Why does Kant think that there are such truths? Why aren't all a priori truths analytic, as Hume claimed? First, consider geometry. Compare the two propositions 'Every triangle has three sides' and 'The angles of a triangle add up to 180 degrees.' The first is analytic; it is true because of the definition of 'triangle.' However, Kant claims that the second is not true by definition. It involves the nature of space. Yet it is a necessary truth. Second, contrast the two statements 'Every effect has a cause' and 'Every event has a cause.' Once again, the first is analytic, because of the meaning of 'effect.' The second is not true by virtue of the definition of 'event.' Therefore, if it is a priori, it is also synthetic. Finally, consider the claims of arithmetic. Kant claims that '7 + 5 =12' is a necessary truth but not analytic. In other words, according to Kant, it is not part of the definition or meaning of '7+5' that it must be equal to 12. Perhaps one can see his insight more easily by considering the following: Is it part of the definition of '7 plus 5' that it equals the cube root of 1728? Kant argues that it is not. '7 + 5 = the cube root of 1728' is not like 'All sisters are female.' One can understand '7+5' without knowing that it is the cube root of 1728, but one cannot understand the word 'sister' without knowing that a sister is a female.

2) The A priori Forms of Experience

Given that there are synthetic a priori truths, we must explain how they are possible. This is why Kant thinks that any possible experience must conform to certain necessary forms. For example, he claims that perceptual experience must be of causally related objects in space and time. Kant tries to deduce such conditions from the nature of consciousness itself. Because consciousness has and must have a certain kind of unity, all experience must be subject to the a priori forms of experience.

3) Transcendental Idealism

How does Kant justify his transcendental idealism? He is certain that we have synthetic a priori knowledge of the world, because geometry is a clear example of it. Kant was also convinced that neither Rationalism nor Empiricism could explain such knowledge. His own answer is to articulate the necessary conditions of any possible experience. But this is not enough. Doing so can at most give us a priori claims about experience. On its own, this could not ensure that the real world conformed to those conditions. Therefore, transcendental idealism must be true. There is no other way to guarantee that the world conforms to the necessary conditions of experience.

The Structure of the Critique

The *Critique* has two major parts, the positive and the negative. In the first, he explains how synthetic a priori truths are possible by developing a non-Empiricist theory of experience. In the second part, the Dialectic, Kant employs this analysis to refute Rationalism. This constitutes a critique of reason by reason.

The first part of the *Critique* has two main sections, the Transcendental Aesthetic and the Analytic of Concepts and Principles. This division reflects Kant's claim that the sensibility (or sensible intuitions) and the understanding (or concepts) are both necessary for experience. Both the faculties of sensibility and the understanding have a priori forms. In the Aesthetic, Kant investigates the a priori forms of sensibility, which are space and time. In the Analytic, he investigates the a priori forms of the understanding, which are the categories. In both the Aesthetic and the Analytic, he defends the two pillars of his explanation of synthetic a priori truths (i.e. premises 1 and 2 above).

By distinguishing intuitions and concepts, Kant transcends the Empiricist and Rationalist traditions. Sensible intuition and the concepts of the understanding are both necessary for experience. Moreover, the difference between the two is one of kind. Kant says that the senses can think nothing and the understanding cannot receive intuitions. Intuitions are the sensory aspect of experience. They are passively received and make it possible for our experience to be of particulars. Concepts are the classificatory or general aspect of experience.

Individually, neither suffices for experience: 'intuitions without concepts are blind; concepts without intuitions are empty.' This is how Kant's theory transcends both Empiricism and Rationalism. Against Empiricism, he claims that intuitions without concepts are blind. This means that sense data or sense impressions without concepts are non-descript. They could not constitute an experience or even be described. Against Rationalism, Kant argues that concepts without intuitions are empty. Apart from their role in experience, concepts have no real meaning. Since both intuitions and concepts are needed for experience, and are blind or empty without each other, we should not think of them as independent elements of experience, but rather as two aspects of experience.

The Transcendental Aesthetic

Experience requires both the senses and the understanding. In the Aesthetic, Kant examines the a priori forms of sensibility. Sensibility is the faculty whereby we passively receive sensible intuitions, which comprise the material for experience. However, this material does not constitute an experience. It must be ordered also by the understanding into a structured experience of spatio-temporal objects.

The main claim of the Aesthetic is that space and time are the a priori forms of sensibility. Experience of objects must be spatial and temporal. Kant has three arguments for this claim. First he argues that space is not an empirical concept derived from experience by abstraction, because in order to represent objects as spatial in the first place, we require an idea of space. Therefore, space is presupposed by our experience of outer objects. Second, he argues that we can imagine empty space, but not the absence of space itself. Kant concludes that space is presupposed by our awareness of outer objects. Third, geometry contains synthetic a priori truths about space, such as 'the angles of a triangle add up to 180 degrees.' Such truths are not empirically known from experience, nor analytically derived from concepts. The only possible explanation of these synthetic necessary truths is that space is a priori.

Kant also claims that space and time are a priori intuitions. This means that they are not relations, as Leibniz claimed. Instead, they are unique infinite individuals; all spaces are parts of the one whole space. However, against Newton, Kant argues that space and time are not absolute entities. They are transcendentally ideal, and not transcendentally real, for otherwise, we could not explain how we have a priori knowledge of them.

Similar points apply to time, except for two differences. First, whereas space is the a priori form of outer intuition, time is the form of inner intuition. In other words, experience itself must be temporal, but external objects must be both spatial and temporal. Second, Kant regarded arithmetic as a body of synthetic a priori truths based on time. Propositions such as '7 + 5=12' are synthetic a priori. They are not analytic because the meanings of '7' and '+5' do not contain the idea of 12. Numbers involve the addition of units, and if arithmetic is to have application to the world, these units must be temporal.

The Analytic of Concepts

Kant calls the a priori concepts of the understanding 'the categories.' For Kant, concepts are the capacity to make judgments of a certain kind. They are rule-governed abilities. This view avoids the problems of the Empiricist treatment of concepts as mental images, namely that to be able to recognize the image of an F as such presupposes that one already has a concept of an F (please replace 'F' with any general terms, such as 'dog').

The Analytic of Concepts has two main sections: the Metaphysical Deduction and the Transcendental Deduction. In the Metaphysical Deduction, Kant tries to isolate candidates for the status of a priori categories. First, he argues that certain concepts are basic because they constitute the forms of judgment. For example, in the judgment 'the coal is black,' the concepts 'coal' and 'black' are the content of the judgment. However, the verb 'is' is not part of that content; it determines the form or structure of the judgment. Second, Kant argues that perceiving is a kind of judging, thereby opposing the Empiricist claim that perception consists solely in passively receiving sense impressions. The categories provide the conceptual form of experience and, therefore, the forms of judgment provide a guide to the categories.

The Transcendental Deduction is the heart of the *Critique*. In the B edition, section 20, Kant argues that the categories are necessary for experience. First, my experiences have to be that of a unified consciousness. Kant calls this formal condition of experience 'the transcendental unity of apperception' (or TUAP). Second, this requirement implies that I should be able to think of my experiences as mine. The unity of consciousness requires the possibility of judging that my experiences are such. Third, the ability to judge that my experiences are mine requires the logical forms of judgment. Therefore, the logical forms of judgment, or the categories, are necessary for experience. In summary, the unity of consciousness requires that experience should be rule-governed and connected by categories. The argument may be represented as follows:

1. All experience must be subject to the T.U.AP.
2. This requires that experience consist in judgments.
3. <u>All judgments must have a form</u>.
4. Therefore, the forms of judgment are necessary conditions of experience.

The Transcendental Unity of Apperception

The TUAP is a formal unity that experience must have. All your experiences belong to one consciousness. When you look out of the window, all aspects of your seeing are united. It is all *your* experience. This formal unity is what makes self-consciousness possible. It makes it possible to think: 'these experiences are mine.' Experience has a unity and, because of this, I can be aware of my experiences as my experiences.

This T.U.AP is not the idea of a self. It is not an entity. It is a structural feature of experience. Kant realizes that, because the unity is required for any experience, it cannot be an object of experience. It is not such an item because it makes all experience possible, including ordinary awareness of oneself and introspection.

Kant's approach to the 'I' is profoundly new. Descartes takes the 'I think' to indicate the existence of a substance, distinct from the body. This ignores an important paradox concerning consciousness, which is that we cannot directly experience it because it constitutes the very having of the experience. Hence, there is the saying: 'the I which sees cannot see itself.' Kant recognizes this paradoxical point and explains it: the 'I' is not an object of possible experience because it is a presupposition of experience.

Hume also rejects Descartes' reification of the 'I,' but according to Kant, Hume's argument leads to an unwarranted skepticism. Hume argues that all concepts must be derived from sense impressions and that there is no sense impression of the 'I.' Consequently, Hume concludes that our concept of the 'I' cannot be justified. Kant rejects this skepticism. He agrees with Hume, against Descartes, that the 'I' cannot be an object of experience. But he disagrees with Hume that this means that the notion of an 'I' cannot be justified. It is justified by being a necessary feature of all awareness.

Objectivity

The Transcendental Deduction contains a second argument (sections 17-19 in the B edition). The first and main argument was given above. The second argument is that the concept of objectivity is a necessary condition of experience. At B142, Kant says that the claim that a judgment is objective means that if it is true, then what it affirms is so, no matter what the state of the subject. Its truth or falsity does not depend on the person. The objectivity of a judgment is expressed by the copula 'is.' This objectivity implies that, for instance, a judgment that an object *is* heavy asserts that the object *is* heavy no matter what the state of the subject.

Kant argues that this concept of objectivity is also a necessary condition of experience. This is because the thought 'I am having this experience' (i.e. the TUAP) requires the distinction between how things seem to be to me and how things objectively are. The thought of subjective experience itself requires the concept of something objective and distinct from experience. In other words, self-consciousness requires the distinction between how things subjectively seem and how they objectively are.

From this point, Kant argues that perceptual experience must be of an objective world consisting of things that exist independently of our perception of them. The idea of an object that exists independently of our perception is a necessary condition of experience.

Kant's account of objectivity is an important philosophical advance. Hume claims both that all concepts must be derived from sense impressions, and that we can only ever perceive our own ideas. Hume notes that the idea of an object that exists independently of my experience cannot be derived from sense impressions. He concludes that such a notion is unjustifiable. In reply, Kant agrees that such a notion cannot be empirically derived from experience, but this is because it is a necessary condition of experience. Objectivity plays an important role in the *Critique*. For example, as we shall see, it is central to Kant's defense of the category of cause.

Now we can see that Kant's Transcendental Deduction constitutes a sustained argument against Empiricism. Experience must have a unity and, thus, Kant rejects the idea of passively received sense impressions. Furthermore, because experience must have a structure, the categories cannot be derived from experience. They are a priori. Hence, not all concepts can be derived from experience.

The Analytic of Principles

In the Principles, Kant shows how each of the 12 categories makes experience possible. As a preliminary, in the Schematism, he argues that the categories need a temporal interpretation to be applicable to experience. Because they are a priori, the categories are not homogeneous with appearances, For example, it is not part of the concept of a cause that causes should look a certain way, unlike, say, the concept of a dog. In reply to this, Kant argues that the categories apply to experience only insofar as they determine the necessary structure of our consciousness of time.

The twelve categories come in four groups of three and so do the Principles, which are the temporalized categories, as listed below. Kant argues that each schematized category is necessary for experience by making objective space and time possible. In this way, they are constitutive of the transcendentally ideal world of things in space and time.

1. The Axioms of Intuition

These correspond to the three categories of quantity: unity, plurality and totality. The corresponding principle claims that all intuitions are extensive magnitudes. Why is mathematics applicable to the natural world? It is not a fortunate accident; indeed the two were made for each other. According to the Axioms, everything in space and time must come under the categories of quantity. Spatial and temporal properties are extensive magnitudes because they can be added. Because of this, they can be represented with numbers and measured. This principle 'alone can make pure mathematics, in its complete precision, applicable to objects of experience' (B206). The world is amenable to being described with mathematical concepts because it is subject to Kant's axiom rather than being a question of luck. The Principle is a synthetic a priori truth: it expresses a condition of experience that the world must conform to. This way the fit is guaranteed.

2. The Anticipations of Perception

This Principle, which corresponds to the three categories of quality (reality, limitation, and negation) states: 'In all appearances, the real that is an object of sensation has intensive magnitude, that is, a degree.' This introduces the idea of degrees of quality, which is not the mathematical concept of extensive magnitude. The qualities of sensations come in degrees that appear continuous, rather than in jumps of discrete units, like extensive magnitudes. Probably, Kant is anticipating the later distinction between cardinal and ordinal measurement (Walker, 1979, p. 95). An ordinal measurement gives a ranking of things without allowing us to quantify the differences between the things so ranked. Whereas cardinal measurements allow us to say the difference between A and B is twice that of C and D, ordinals do not. Clearly Kant's extensive magnitudes are cardinal. The point now is that intensive magnitudes are ordinal.

3. The Postulates of Empirical Thought

These Principles correspond to the three categories of modality: necessary, actual and possible. Let us start with the actual: 'something is actual if it connects with some actual perception in the accordance with the analogies' (A225). This shows that the actual does not have to be perceived. Unseen distant galaxies and tiny electrons are still actual. They can be causally connected to an actual perception and thus belong to the same world, in the same unified space and time.

Given the definition of the actual, those concerning the necessary and possible are easier to follow. By 'possible,' Kant means causally possible, as opposed to logically possible. Many things that are logically possible are not causally possible. For example, it is logically possible that a person might jump over a huge building, although this is not causally possible. In this sense, the possible is defined in terms of the Analogies. Similar points apply to the notion of necessary; the causally necessary should be distinguished from the logically necessary.

4. The Analogies

These principles correspond to the three categories of relation: substance, cause and reciprocity. The analogies are the most important of the principles. They specify the ways events in the world are connected to make objective time and space possible.

1. The First Analogy

Kant tries to prove that, in all change, substance is permanent. This means that all changes are alterations to the properties of substance and that the amount of substance cannot change. The First Analogy is a synthetic a priori truth. It gives us information about the world, but it is a necessary truth. Kant's argument has four steps. First, the unity of experience requires the distinction between the subjective and objective and, therefore, we must be able to distinguish the subjective time sequence of our perceptions from the objective sequence of events. Second, objective judgments about when real changes occur cannot be made in relation to absolute time, which is not an object of possible experience. Third, as a result, there has to be some permanent aspect of experience so that judgments about the objective timing of events make sense, and this is substance. Therefore, the category of substance is necessary for experience. Fourth, according to transcendental idealism, all events in the phenomenal world must conform to the categories, because otherwise they would not be objects of possible experience. Therefore, all events conform to the principle of the permanency of substance. Thus, no change can count as the creation or destruction of substance.

2. The Second Analogy

The principle 'All events must have a cause' is synthetic a priori because 'cause' is a necessary condition of experience. Again, the argument for this conclusion has four steps. First, the unity of consciousness requires that we can distinguish a subjective succession of perceptions from a perception of objective change. Second, the idea of an objective change requires the concept of the lack of order indifference of perceptions. For example, when I perceive the movement of a boat downstream, my perceptions lack this feature of order indifference. To be the perception of a series of events, the perceptions must have a certain order. In contrast, when I perceive the coexistent parts of a house, my perceptions could occur in any order. Third, the lack of order indifference requires that the appropriate changes are caused. Therefore, causation is necessary for experience. Fourth, the transcendentally ideal world must conform to the necessary conditions of experience and, thus, all events are caused. Any event without a cause could not be experienced. Accordingly, the argument is as follows:

1. The distinction between the subjective sequence of perceptions and the objective sequence of events is a necessary condition of any experience.
2. This distinction can only be made empirically in relation to the necessary order of perceptions.
3. If the order of our perceptions of a change is necessary, then the <u>order of the change itself is causally determined</u>.
4. Therefore, causation is a necessary condition of any experience.

From this conclusion, given that the world must conform to the necessary conditions of experience (i.e. transcendental idealism), we can deduce that all events are caused. Any event without a cause could not be experienced. Therefore, all events must have a cause. In the above argument, premise 1 is a conclusion of the Transcendental

Deduction. Kant argues for premise 2, by claiming that neither absolute time itself nor the mere order of our perceptions are adequate to make the required distinction.

Objective time is made possible by causation. Suppose that E1 occurs before E2. We cannot think of that objective determination in relation to Newtonian absolute time. However, cause makes that determination possible, because a cause cannot come after its effect. E1 is before E2 if and only if either E1 causes or is simultaneous with the cause of E2 (simultaneity is the topic of the Third Analogy). Cause-effect makes 'before-after' possible. The direction of time is made possible by the irreversible and asymmetric nature of the causal relation.

The Second Analogy is an extended reply to Hume's skepticism about cause. Hume's skepticism is based on his two epistemological principles: the theory of ideas and Hume's fork (see Chapter 15). First, Hume claims that the idea of a necessary causal connection cannot be derived from sense impressions and, hence, cannot be justified. In reply, Kant argues that the notion of cause is not derived from experience because it is a necessary condition of experience. Second, the essence of Hume's fork is that it only offers two alternatives: either propositions are a priori and analytic, or else they are synthetic and empirical. Hume notes that the principle 'Every event must have a cause' fits into neither of these two options, and he concludes that it cannot be justified. However, Kant rejects Hume's fork. He replaces it with a trident, arguing for a third alternative, synthetic a priori truths, and thereby tries to rescue causation from Hume's skepticism.

Empirical Realism and Transcendental Idealism

Kant is an empirical realist because he denies that we can perceive only our own ideas and he claims that the spatio-temporal objects that we perceive exist independently of our perception of them. As we saw earlier, the concept of objectivity is a necessary condition of experience.

At the same time, Kant is a transcendental idealist because the categories and space and time only have meaningful application to the objects of possible experience. Thus, he claims that spatio-temporal objects are necessarily relative to and subject to the a priori forms of experience. He expresses this transcendental idealism by claiming that objects in space and time are phenomenal and not noumenal. By 'phenomenal,' he means relative to the a priori conditions of any experience. By 'noumenal' he means absolute, and not relative to those conditions. Thus, he claims that 'noumena' is an empty limiting concept.

The Refutation of Empirical Idealism

The refutation of empirical idealism is at the same time a vindication of empirical realism. Kant argues that, in perception, we are directly aware of external objects, which exist independently of our perceptions of them. Thus, he denies that we can only be directly aware of our own ideas. Kant denies that knowledge of our own experiences is more certain than that of the external world, by arguing that we can only be aware of our own experiences if we are directly aware of external objects. Kant's main point is that any inner state can have an objective date only in relation to a framework of relatively permanent outer things. No experience can have an objective date in relation to other inner states. Objective time requires outer objects. The argument is as follows:

1. I am conscious of my own experiences in time
2. All time perceptions require something permanent in perception.
3. This permanent is either a perceptual experience or external objects that are not perceptions.
4. The permanent in perception cannot be a perceptual experience.
5. Therefore, the perception of outer objects is a necessary condition of self-consciousness.

The crux of the argument is premise 2. The point is that inner states can have temporal dates only in relation to a permanent framework of outer things. Premise 4 asserts that any permanent perception itself requires an objective position in time, and so it requires something permanent that is distinct from any perception itself. In other words, an experience or inner state cannot have a determinate date merely in relation to other inner states.

With this argument, Kant says that he has turned the game played by idealists against itself. Idealism assumes that the knowledge of our own inner experiences is more certain than any belief we could have about the external world. Kant rejects the heart of this assumption by arguing that we can only be aware of our own experiences if we are directly aware of external objects. The existence and knowledge of things outside me is necessary for my awareness of my own experience. Kant tries to bury Descartes' assumption that the experiences of a solipsistic mind would be indistinguishable from a mind that perceived objects.

Kant's empirical realism constitutes the first step in a transformation of our understanding that reached its fruition only in the 20th century. We are part of this shared public world and, not individuals caught in a solipsistic private world of our own mental states. However, it is debatable to what extent Kant appreciated the full implications of this aspect of this own philosophy.

Transcendental Idealism

Transcendental idealism is the claim that objects in space and time are transcendentally ideal. In other words, things in space and time are phenomenal and not noumenal. This means that they are relative to and subject to the necessary conditions of any possible experience rather than being noumenal or absolute.

Kant has three arguments for transcendental idealism. First, the categories have no meaning apart from their role in providing the structure of experience. Therefore, they have no sense except in relation to objects of possible experience and cannot be meaningfully employed to describe an absolute or noumenal reality. Second, things in space and time must be relative to the necessary conditions of experience because otherwise they could not be experienced at all. In other words, empirical realism requires transcendental idealism. Third, if transcendental idealism were not true, then it would be impossible to explain how synthetic a priori truths are possible. Such truths can only be explained on the assumption that the world necessarily conforms to the necessary conditions of experience and that assumption is transcendental idealism.

Transcendental idealism indicates a condition or relativity in our notions of objects and reality. This implies that the world is not absolute: it does not consist of things as they are in themselves, without reference to any conditions. In other words, the world is not noumenal.

Furthermore, the notion of the noumenal is empty. The necessary conditions of experience are the parameters of meaning. Any claim to metaphysical knowledge that goes beyond those boundaries will be senseless. This is because the categories have no meaning except in relation to possible experience. Therefore, noumena do not form a reality separate from things in space and time. The idea of things as they are noumenally, that is as they are without reference to the necessary conditions of experience, is the idea of an absolute viewpoint on things. But this idea is merely an empty limiting concept. Kant says that the noumenal leaves 'open a space which we can fill neither through possible experience nor pure understanding' (A289/B345).

This means that we should not think of noumena as non-spatio-temporal objects. Noumena are not an unknowable realm of objects beyond space and time. To think in that way would be to fall into the error of metaphysics. Noumena and phenomena are not two different realms of reality. There is only one world, namely things in space and time. There are two viewpoints on it: the normal viewpoint of possible experience, the phenomenal, and a God's eye or absolute viewpoint, i.e. the noumenal. The latter is no more than the empty idea of the unconditioned.

Transcendental idealism has two important roles in Kant's philosophy. First, it explains how we can know a priori that the world actually conforms to the necessary conditions of experience, which is vital for explaining synthetic a priori truths. Second, it prescribes the limits of knowledge; space and time and the categories only have meaning in relation to the objects of possible experience, i.e. to phenomena and not to noumena. This is the basis for Kant's attack on metaphysics in the Dialectic.

The Reconciliation

How is Kant's empirical realism compatible with his transcendental idealism? The two are compatible because claiming that the form of the world depends on the form of any possible experience does not make the world dependent on perceivers or perceptions. There is an important difference between affirming:

A. The formal character of objects depends on the formal character of any possible experience, and
B. Objects depend for their existence on perceivers.

A, unlike B, does not make the existence of objects depend on any perceivers. According to statement A, spatio-temporal objects would still exist even if there were no perceivers. According to statement B, they would not. A is compatible with Kant's objectivity thesis and his empirical realism; B is not. A says that the notion of reality is relative to certain conditions. B asserts that it is relative to perceivers. In summary, Kant's transcendental idealism claims that the spatio-temporal world is objective, but not absolute.

Given this explanation, we can see the difference between Kant and Berkeley. Kant asserts (and Berkeley denies) that objects exist independently of our perceptions. And Berkeley asserts (and Kant denies) that we can only perceive our own ideas. For this reason, Kant claims to be an empirical realist; spatio–temporal objects are real. They are objectively real, because they do not depend on us for their existence. They are transcendentally ideal because they are relative to the necessary conditions of experience.

Questions of Interpretation

Ever since the *Critique* first came off the printing press, many readers have interpreted Kant's idealism to be very similar to Berkeley's. Kant's rewrote the *Critique* for the B edition partly to avoid this reading. According to the strong Berkeley-like interpretation of transcendental idealism, (a) reality consists in non spatio-temporal noumena, and (b) phenomenal objects in space and time, or appearances, are merely products or constructs of human experience. Our knowledge is confined to phenomena.

This strong interpretation is very different from the milder one that I have explained. The strong version claims that noumena are objects; the milder one denies this. The strong interpretation affirms that phenomenal objects are really subjective ideas; the mild version denies that.

The strong reading conflicts with two of the central aims of the *Critique*. First, it implies that noumena are real. To think that reality consists in non spatio-temporal noumena requires us to apply the categories beyond the bounds of possible experience. Kant's criticism of Rationalism is precisely that one cannot do that. Second, the strong interpretation denies the objectivity thesis and empirical realism. If objects in space and time are merely constructs from human experience, then they are not objective. However, as we have seen, the objectivity of claims about the spatio-temporal world is a major theme running throughout the *Critique*. Therefore, if we can avoid this strong interpretation of Kant, then we should do so. It conflicts with important and central parts of the first *Critique*.

Having said that, it should be noted that many passages of the *Critique* suggest the stronger reading. For this reason, historically, most readers of Kant up to the late 20th century have assumed a strong reading of transcendental idealism. As a consequence, sadly, the history of philosophy is littered with what is possibly a misreading of Kant.

The Transcendental Dialectic

The first half of the *Critique of Pure Reason* has explained how a priori knowledge of the world is possible and from this Kant has developed a theory of experience opposed to Empiricism. Also, Kant has argued for the principle that he needs for his critique of Rationalist metaphysics in the second half of the *Critique*: it is impossible to have knowledge that transcends the bounds of possible experience because, beyond that, the categories have no sense. This is the basis of his critique of metaphysics. In claiming to have a priori knowledge of the soul, God, and the universe as a whole, the Rationalists try to apply the categories beyond the limits of possible experience.

The Dialectic is also a critique by reason of itself. Reason is the faculty that makes inferences. Reason is led to the Ideas of the unconditioned, such as God, because it searches for a complete explanation of everything and thus searches for the unconditioned, which is not an object of possible experience. To remedy this error, the Dialectic also describes the proper function of reason. Briefly, the Ideas of Reason lay down heuristic maxims, which only serve to guide investigation. The error is to suppose that these maxims give us a priori knowledge of the world. In other words, synthetic a priori truths are possible in science and mathematics precisely because they articulate the necessary conditions both of experience and of a transcendentally ideal world. Synthetic a priori truths in metaphysics are not possible because they do not do this. Kant shows that the Ideas of Reason satisfy neither of those two conditions.

The Paralogisms

Descartes tries to prove the existence of a non-physical substance, the soul, on the basis of the 'I think.' Kant opposes this, claiming that the 'I think' is just the formal unity of consciousness. The Transcendental Unity of Apperception cannot be an object of experience, because every experience must be subject to this unity and, therefore, it cannot designate any object or self. Descartes is mistaking a formal feature of experience for the awareness of a substance, the soul.

The four Paralogisms are fallacious arguments that apparently support Descartes' rational psychology. The first affirms that the 'I' is a substance. Kant says this affirmation rests on an empty notion of substance. The concept of substance can only have meaningful application to objects of possible experience. However, the 'I think' is not such an object. Thus, to assert that the 'I' is a substance is to make an empty statement, which we cannot use to prove the immortality of the soul, or to distinguish the self from matter, contrary to what Descartes supposed.

The second Paralogism asserts that the soul is a simple. The actions of a simple cannot be regarded as the actions of an aggregate. The soul apparently fits this bill. But, as before, Kant rejects this argument on the grounds that the transcendental unity of consciousness does not designate an object and, therefore, does not refer to a simple.

Descartes confuses the unity of consciousness with the richer idea of a simple soul.

The third Paralogism asserts that a person is that which is conscious of its numerical identity through time, and that the soul is such a thing. Kant replies that the claim that the soul is conscious of its numerical identity through time merely expresses the necessary unity of consciousness. This unity of consciousness is not an object. Hence, the claim that the subject is numerically identical through time is empty. In fact, at A363, Kant says that even if there were soul substances, there could be no guarantee that a person might not consist of as many souls as he has experiences rather than one soul. There can be no guarantee that one person has only one soul. The point here is that the notion of an identical soul can not work, because it contains no criteria for identity, unlike the notion of a spatio-temporal object. My experience could inhere in 2000 souls, but the experience would still be mine because it is subject to the Transcendental Unity of Apperception.

The Antinomies

The Antinomies consist of a thesis and an antithesis, which are apparently contradictory propositions that can be supported by equally valid proofs. The arguments for both the thesis and antithesis assume a certain view of Reason. The contradiction shows us that we must reject the assumed view of Reason, which implies transcendental realism. Once we adopt transcendental idealism, the antinomies are dissolved.

For example, in the first antinomy, the thesis claims that the world is finite both in space and time because a completed infinity is impossible. The antithesis argues that the universe must be infinite in space and time because a finite universe cannot be explained. In both arguments, Reason demands the existence of the unconditioned on the grounds that, if the conditioned is given, then the unconditioned is also given. Reason demands a complete explanation of any event, and postulates the unconditioned. However, the unconditioned can never be experienced and, thus, is empty and, given this point, the antinomy can be diffused. We can replace this faulty view of Reason with one that regards Reason as setting us an indefinite task, rather than making an imposition on the world. Reason sets a directive, rather than making a claim as to what exists.

The problem and solution of the second Antinomy is similar to the first. The thesis claims that simples, or indivisible atoms, exist. It is impossible for a composite to be made up of aggregates which are themselves made up of aggregates and so on without end. Therefore, there must be indivisible simples. The antithesis argues for the impossibility of composites being made up of simples, because every part of a composite occupies space, and space is infinitely divisible. Anything that occupies space is infinitely divisible and cannot be made up of simples (see Chapter 13).

Both arguments assume that there must be something unconditioned. The thesis argues that it must consist of simple atoms, because a completed infinity is impossible. The antithesis contends that it must consist of the infinitely divisible because simples are impossible. Kant's solution to the Second Antinomy is to reject the claim that the unconditioned could exist i.e. to deny the assumption that matter in space is given either as a finitely or as an infinitely divisible whole. Matter in space is indefinitely divisible and presents us with an endless task of investigation. Once again, this endless task of investigation should not be confused with a task of investigating the endless (Strawson, 1966).

Freedom

In the third Antinomy, Kant tries to reconcile the doctrine of determinism with the idea of freedom. On the one hand, every event must have a cause; on the other hand, it is a precondition of morality that our actions are free.

Kant claims that this apparent contradiction can be resolved. The solution is that we can regard our actions in two ways: first, as causally determined phenomena and secondly, as noumena that do not belong to the spatio-temporal world. As rational beings susceptible to moral imperatives, we must regard ourselves as noumena. Because we can regard our actions and ourselves in these two ways, the doctrine of determinism and the idea of freedom can be reconciled and the Third Antinomy can be solved. We shall return to this reconciliation in the next chapter.

God

The third section of the Dialectic and the fourth Antinomy both concern the ideal of Reason, God. Like that of freedom, the idea of God is the idea of the unconditioned. The unconditioned can never be met with in experience and, therefore, it is not an object in the phenomenal world. However, Kant is not merely denying the possibility of knowledge; he is denying meaning. The categories have meaning only in relation to objects of possible experience. Apart from that role, they have no sense; they are empty (B707). Therefore, the mistake of traditional theology is to use the categories without sense.

Kant explains the specific Idea of God in terms of an unconditioned Idea of reality as a totality. Any particular thing is determinate with respect to all pairs of contradictory predicates; either it is red or not red, round or not etc. This principle that all things are completely determinate requires the idea of all possible predicates (A572), as opposed to the predicates we know. It requires the unconditioned idea of a complete totality, or the sum of all reality. This unconditioned idea leads to the ideal of a thing containing all of realities, which Kant calls the *ens realissimum*. This ideal is our concept of God, the only really complete thing (A576).

Kant criticizes three arguments for God's existence. He attacks the ontological argument on the grounds that existence is not a predicate or property (A 626). There is no difference between the idea of a God who exists and the idea of a God who does not exist. Existence adds nothing to the idea of God, and so existence cannot be a perfect quality (see Chapter 4). He says that the claim 'God is a necessary being' does not imply that God necessarily exists. It only means that if God exists then a necessary being exists. It is compatible with this to deny that God exists.

The cosmological argument is as follows: if anything contingent exists, then something necessary must exist; something contingent does exist, and so does the necessary, which must be God. Kant concentrates on the last part of this argument, that is, on the step from 'something necessary exists' to 'God exists.' He claims that this last step presupposes the ontological argument. This last step involves two assertions: first, that if anything is a necessary being then it is God and, second, that if anything is God then it is a necessary being. Kant claims that this second assertion involves the ontological argument and as such is invalid.

The physico-theological argument is often called 'the argument from design.' Kant says that the order in nature does not show the need for a creator, or for a designer. Furthermore, the argument from design presupposes the cosmological argument, because the former moves from an order in nature to the existence of a necessary being, and hence God. Having already rejected the cosmological argument and the notion of necessary existence, Kant also rejects the argument from design.

Conclusion

In summary, Kant's main aim is to give a non-empiricist argument against Rationalism. Synthetic a priori judgments in science and mathematics are justified by two conditions: the necessary structure of experience and transcendental idealism. Traditional metaphysics fails to satisfy these two conditions. Metaphysics is impossible, not because it fails the two prongs of Hume's fork, but because it fails the third prong of Kant's trident, the synthetic a priori. Intuitions without concepts are blind and, therefore, Empiricism is false. Concepts without intuitions are empty and, therefore, Rationalism is false.

21

Kant: From Theory to Practice

According to the *Critique of Pure Reason,* science requires the empty idea of the unconditioned or the noumenal. This is because science relies on synthetic a priori claims, which can be explained only on the assumption that the universe is conditional on the necessary forms of experience. In other words, the world of objects in space and time is not absolute, but is transcendentally ideal, and this requires the negative notion of noumena. These points do not vindicate traditional metaphysics. On the contrary, they condemn it to senselessness because theoretical concepts have sense only in application to the objects of possible experience. Therefore, theoretical concepts have no meaning when applied to the ideas of the unconditional or the noumenal.

Nevertheless, this theoretically empty notion of the noumenal is the key to Kant's morality. In his ethics, Kant makes explicit the Enlightenment notion of a person as an autonomous being capable of free rational choices. This is the very basis of his ethics and his political theory. However, such a notion seems incompatible with the scientific mechanical description of the universe, as exemplified by Kant's second analogy. Furthermore, how can the notion of unconditional freedom be meaningful given Kant's argument against metaphysics? His answer is that the empty notion of the noumenal required by theory becomes converted into the morally meaningful idea of freedom precisely because freedom is a requirement of morality. Before we explain this, we need to review Kant's ethical theory.

Kant's Ethics

The main aim of Kant's *The Groundwork of the Metaphysics of Morals* (1785) is to explain and justify the inescapable nature of moral claims. He distinguishes hypothetical and categorical imperatives. Hypothetical imperatives specify the means to some end. Because they are conditional on an end, such imperatives are escapable. We can escape them by giving up the relevant end. In contrast, moral demands are inescapable and thus consist in a Categorical Imperative of the unconditional form: 'You ought to do Y.'

Kant's main aim in the *Groundwork* is to explain how the Categorical Imperative is possible. His question is 'How is the inescapable nature of morality possible?' Kant's answer is that the categorical demand of morality is inherent in our being persons with free will. This capacity for freely choosing our actions, Kant calls practical reason. Morality is inherent in the form of practical reason and this is why we cannot escape the demands of morality.

Kant argues that, to explain the Categorical Imperative, he must isolate the a priori element of morality. The Categorical Imperative cannot be derived empirically from experience or from human nature, because such empirical factors cannot explain the essentially inescapable nature of morality. Therefore, Kant claims that he must give a deduction of, or transcendental argument for, the a priori form of morality. This does not mean that human nature and the circumstances of our lives are morally unimportant. It only means that these empirical factors cannot explain why moral claims are inescapable. In fact, Kant discusses the application of morality to human life in the later work, the *Metaphysics of Morals* (1797). According to this work, applied morality does depend on various empirical factors, including human nature. For the moment, in the *Groundwork*, Kant is only concerned with the a priori form of morality, in order to explain why it is inescapable.

Kant's distinction between hypothetical and categorical imperatives undermines Hume's skeptical moral theory. According to Hume, many of our fundamental convictions concerning our ideas of cause, object and self cannot be justified. Hume gives a naturalistic explanation of these ideas, which is based on the emotive side of human nature, rather than on the rational (see Chapter 16). Hume's view of morality follows a similar pattern. 'Ought' judgments cannot be justified, but they can be explained in terms of sympathy. Morality is based on a feeling of sympathy (see Chapter 16).

Kant sees problems with this type of view. For example, suppose I do not feel sympathy. In such a case, Hume's position seems to imply that I am not under any obligations to avoid harming you. If morality is based on sympathy, then people who lack a feeling of sympathy are not under any moral obligations. Furthermore, if morality is so based, then there can be no sense to the claim 'I ought to feel more sympathy.' Kant argues that Hume's theory turns morality into a system of escapable hypothetical imperatives.

The Will and Ordinary Morality

In the first chapter of the *Groundwork*, Kant tries to show that the Categorical Imperative is already part of our everyday morality. The basis of popular morality is the will. He argues that the moral worth of an action does not depend on its effects or consequences. In part, this is because the will, by definition, is under our own control, whereas the effects of our actions depend on factors beyond our control. Furthermore, a morally right action must be done for the morally right motive. A good will must act for the sake of duty. Actions that happen to accord with duty are different from those that are actually motivated by it. In short, Kant claims that only the good will is good without qualification. The moral worth of other things, such as intelligence and happiness, depend on it.

The Deduction of the Categorical Imperative

In the second chapter of the *Groundwork*, Kant tries to demonstrate four different versions of the Categorical Imperative. The first version states:

1) Universal Law: *Act on that maxim through which you can at the same time will that it should become a universal law.* The Categorical Imperative cannot prescribe action for the sake of any specific empirical ends because that would convert it into a hypothetical imperative. Consequently, the only end that it can recommend is the universality of law as such. Initially, the only thing that reason can recommend is rationality itself. This abstract principle rules out inconsistent willing. I cannot will that other people should not lie to me, and will that I can lie to them. There are two kinds of inconsistent willing ruled out in this way. First, some maxims strictly cannot be universalized. For example, it is impossible to universalize the following maxim: I will borrow money, but not repay it. If

everyone had that maxim, money-lending institutions would collapse. This kind of maxim generates perfect duties - acts that one must not perform at any time. Second, some universalized maxims are not strictly self-contradictory, but they are inconsistent with natural ends that a rational person would will, such as the development of one's talents. These maxims generate imperfect duties - acts that in general one should perform.

2) Respect for Persons: *Act in such a way that you always treat humanity, whether in your own person or that of another, never simply as a means but always at the same time as an end.* In other words, we must respect persons by never using them merely as instruments for some goal, for example by manipulating them. We should respect the fact that persons are beings with free will. This version of the Imperative follows from the first, because the will must be determined by an end, which must be valid for all rational beings as such and, therefore, is not based on any desire. This end must be rational nature itself, and rational nature cannot be merely a means.

3) Autonomy: *So act that your will can regard itself at the same time as making universal law through its maxims.* This formulation introduces the person as a law-maker, or as an autonomous being. The second version postulated rational nature as an end in itself, but rational nature is the capability to will freely, which is the capacity to act according to self-made laws. Thus, if a being is rational, then he or she is a law-maker.

4) Kingdom of Ends: *Act on the maxim of a member who makes universal law for a merely possible kingdom of ends.* The idea is that each member of a community of persons should regard his or her maxims as making a law that would govern the actions of all the other members too. Only in this way can a community of rational beings treat one another as ends. This version of the Categorical Imperative is the basis of Kant's political philosophy.

The Moral Deduction

Having explained the different versions of the Categorical Imperative, Kant gives a transcendental argument to show how the Categorical Imperative is possible. The basis of this argument is the claim that if we are beings with a free will, then the Categorical Imperative applies to us without exception. The overall argument in the *Groundwork* is as follows:

Argument A:

1. If we are beings with a free will, then the Categorical Imperative applies to us without exception.
2. We are beings with a free will.
3. The Categorical Imperative applies to us without exception

Kant's argument for the first premise comes in three steps. The first step is that beings with a free will must also have practical reason or, in other words, that its actions can be guided by reasons or principles. Second, that we are capable of being moved by reason implies that we are capable of acting in accord with the Categorical Imperative. The third step is to show that if the Categorical Imperative is possible, then it is binding on us. The Categorical Imperative cannot lay down any particular empirical ends because such ends would only generate hypothetical imperatives. The only end that could be recommended by the Categorical Imperative is rationality itself.

Argument B:

1. If we are beings with a free will, then we have practical reason
2. If we have practical reason, then the Categorical Imperative is possible for us
3. If the Categorical Imperative is possible for us then it applies to us without exception.
4. If we are beings with a free will, then the Categorical Imperative applies to us without exception

In summary, Kant's moral philosophy revolves around free will in three ways. First, we are under the inescapable moral obligation of the Categorical Imperative, because this is inherent in our being free. Second, the essence of morality is that we will in accordance with morality's demand. Third, it demands that we should respect the freedom of persons. In other words, morality applies to us because we have a will and it directs our will to respect the will.

From Theory to Practice

Kant's deduction of morality is not yet complete. The argument so far has shown that *if* we are beings with a free will, then the Categorical Imperative applies to us. However, Kant has not yet argued that we *are* free beings, i.e. for premise 2 of argument of A above.

In fact, in the third chapter of the *Groundwork*, Kant is careful *not* to assert that we know ourselves to have a free will. We cannot assert such theoretical knowledge, because freedom is an idea of Reason to which nothing in the natural world can ever correspond. Knowledge is necessarily confined to the objects of possible experience. Therefore, in the *Groundwork,* Kant merely claims to derive morality from the will, but he does not argue for the claim that we have free will. In this derivation, freedom of the will has to be presupposed.

The problem is graver than the above suggests, because the idea of noumenal freedom has no real meaning insofar as that the categories only make sense only in application to the objects of possible experience. However, Kant tries to solve this problem in the *Critique of Practical Reason* (1788). In the second *Critique*, Kant tries to show that the claim that we are free can be justified on moral grounds. The idea of freedom must have meaning because it is a requirement of moral practice. Indeed, that is its meaning and it can have no other.

This new approach allows Kant to argue that morality transforms the otherwise empty noumenal idea of the unconditioned will. Although the idea of freedom has no meaning in relation to possible experience, it must have a different kind of content in relation to the practice of morality. In other words, the idea of a noumenal will is a vacant hole left by theory, but it is filled in by moral understanding.

In conclusion, in the *Groundwork*, Kant tries to deduce the a priori nature of morality from the idea of the free will. In contrast, in the second *Critique*, he tries to justify the idea of freedom in terms of morality. He tries to show how our otherwise empty idea of noumenal freedom must have a meaning in relation to moral practice.

Religion as an Extension of Morality

At the beginning of the first *Critique*, Kant says that he abolishes knowledge to make room for faith (Bxxx). As we shall see, it would have been more accurate to say that he abolishes theoretical meaning and knowledge to make room for practical meaning and knowledge.

To repeat an earlier point, in the first *Critique,* Kant affirms that the notion of noumena is only an empty concept because we cannot meaningfully apply the categories beyond the realm of possible experience. Therefore, Kant's critique of Rationalism is not that metaphysics tries to make knowledge-claims about an unknowable noumenal realm. Rather, his reproach is that metaphysics has no real sense because it involves using the categories beyond the bounds of possible experience. This critique applies also to the theological ideas of God and the soul.

In the second *Critique*, Kant tries to show how these theological ideas of the unconditioned can have a practical content in relation to moral practice, in much the same way that the idea of freedom does. Because freedom of the will is a requirement of morality, the idea of unconditioned freedom acquires a practical meaning in relation to ethics. He now argues that this meaning can be extended to the religious ideas of God and the immortal soul, because they too are an implicit requirement of morality. In other words, regarding the idea of God, he argues

1. Ideas of the noumenal have practical sense if and only if they are a requirement of moral practice.
2. The idea of God is a requirement of moral practice.
3. Therefore, it has practical sense.

To understand premise 2, we must look at Kant's notion of the *summum bonum,* or the perfect good. The ideal of the perfect good contains a union of two elements: virtue and happiness. Virtue is good, but it is better to be virtuous and happy. Similarly, happiness is better when it is deserved because of virtue.

However, according to Kant, the connection between virtue and happiness is synthetic a priori. It is synthetic, and not analytic, because the one idea is not contained in the other. However, it is a priori, not empirical, because virtue does not always bring happiness, and happy people are not always virtuous. The claim that virtue ideally ought to cause happiness is a *practical* synthetic a priori claim. It is not a *theoretical* synthetic a priori truth, because it does not state a necessary condition of experience.

Please note that Kant is not claiming that we should be moral because, in the long run, this shall make us happy. Such a claim would contradict the very fundamentals of his moral philosophy. Although justice requires that virtue should bring happiness, moral virtue is valuable for its own sake.

The *summum bonum*, or the perfect good, is the ideal of practical reason. Therefore, because we are subject to the Categorical Imperative, we must believe that this ideal is attainable. Given this point, as we shall now see, Kant derives the ideas of an immortal soul and God.

a) God guarantees the synthetic and a priori connection between virtue and happiness. The idea of God as an all-good being is required for the idea that happiness should be proportioned according to virtue, as justice requires. In other words, belief in God is inherent in our moral understanding and practice. Belief that the moral ideal of the *summum bonum* is attainable implicitly requires belief in God. Therefore, pursuit of the highest good justifies the idea of God. Kant does not mean that moral reasons depend on God. Kant's claim is rather that the idea of God is implicit in our moral practices and ideals and that, in this way, the otherwise empty idea of God acquires a moral significance.

b) In a similar way, the idea of the immortal soul is also a practical precondition of morality only, in this case, the relevant ideal is that of perfect virtue. We must think that the ideal of perfect virtue is attainable. Perfect virtue presents itself to us as an endless task of progressing towards the ideal. Therefore, the ideal requires immortality, 'the unending duration of the existence and personality of the same rational being' (220). To deny this requirement would effectively be to deny that the ideal can be attained and this denial, argues Kant, is equivalent to denying the ideal itself.

In summary, in the second *Critique*, Kant argues for three postulates of practical reason. The first is that morality requires that we must regard ourselves as noumenal beings free from causal laws. The second postulate is that morality requires that we must regard ourselves as having an immortal soul. The third is that morality requires that we must regard God as existing. The second and third postulates are indirect requirements of morality, because they depend on moral ideals. The first is direct.

Practical and not Theoretical Meaning

According to Kant, none of this means that we actually can affirm that God exists or that we have an immortal soul. The criticisms of Rationalist metaphysics, given in the Dialectic of the first *Critique*, still stand. Traditional metaphysics is mistaken in thinking that such ideas have theoretical meaning.

However, Kant's new point in the second *Critique* is that these ideas of the unconditioned have practical content. This implies we have moral reasons to view the universe and act as though God exists etc. If we did not view the universe and ourselves in these ways, then we would be involved in an inconsistency with regard to morality. We ought to strive for moral ideals. In such striving, we presuppose that these ideals are attainable, and this presupposition requires the ideas of God and an immortal soul. God is implicit in the striving. For this reason, Kant calls a practical postulate no more than a 'practically necessary hypothesis' (11-12). In other words, the three postulates of practical reason do not amount to a theoretical defense of free will, of an immortal soul and of a just God.

The distinction between theoretical and practical meaning is very delicate. Suppose that we ask Kant 'Does God exist?' His first answer would be 'The *assertion* that God exists does not make sense because such an assertion would amount to a theoretical metaphysical claim that tries to transcend the bounds of possible experience.' His second reply would be 'However, I ought to strive for moral ideals, such as justice, and in this striving the idea of God is presupposed.'

In summary, Kant does not argue for the existence of two realms, the phenomenal and noumenal. He is not an ontological dualist. Everything that exists is part of the phenomenal world of things in space and time. Nevertheless, he argues for two kinds of meaning and knowledge, the theoretical and practical. The meaning of theoretical concepts is derived from their role in possible experience. The content of practical ideas is derived from their role in moral practice. These practical ideas cannot be justified in theoretical terms because, from the theoretical point of view, the idea of noumena can be no more than an empty limiting idea. However, as a consequence of their practical content, some of the claims of religion have a moral sense. In this way, religion depends on morality.

From Ethics to Politics

For Kant, politics is the social application of the Categorical Imperative. The fundamental principle of politics is that the will of one person can be unified with the will of another under a universal law of freedom. In application to the state, this principle requires a 'constitution allowing the greatest possible human freedom in accordance with laws which ensure the freedom of each can coexist with the freedom of all the others.' In this way, it is a condition of political freedom that there be an enforced law. Freedom requires some coercion. In other words, freedom implies that it is morally legitimate to use coercion, on the basis of the law, against someone who infringes the freedom of others. Any other type of coercion is wrong.

Social Contract

The function and justification of the state is to preserve that individual autonomy through a common law. As rational beings, we must treat ourselves as ends and as autonomous law-makers. Consequently, all societal laws must be ones that the people would agree to, and all laws must be made public. Anything else would contradict our autonomous nature. For this reason, the state can be justified in terms of a social contract.

However, Kant does not regard the social contract as a historical fact, as Rousseau and Locke tend to, but rather as a practical idea of

Reason. The social contract is a moral ideal, according to which people *should* be willing to submit their individual will to the universal will. The universal will is not the will of the majority, as it seems to be for Rousseau. Rather, it is an idea of reason, which justifies government by law.

The problem of many social contract theories is that they are stuck in a dilemma. On the one hand, if there really had been a binding social contract, then it might justify the state. However, we know that the idea of a social contract is a historical fiction. On the other hand, the idea of a purely hypothetical social contract, one that could have been made but never was, does not seem to justify anything i.e. one is not bound by a promise that one never made. Kant escapes this dilemma by arguing that a social contract is a moral ideal inherent in universal reason. It is what we all ought to agree to. Theoretically, this means that the state is justified morally and not in terms of expediency. In practice, this norm implies that the legislator should apply the test of universalizability to the laws in question.

According to Kant, the establishment of a state is a requirement of reason or of the Categorical Imperative itself. The right to freedom of each should be protected by a system of universal law according to the social contract. The idea of the social contract requires a constitution for establishing the state, and this in turn should specify a separation of powers. In these terms, Kant defines a republican form of government. It requires the distinction between legislature, executive and judiciary. In making this separation, Kant is not arguing against all monarchies. However, he claims that sovereign authority resides with the people, which could be put into practice through a legislative representative assembly.

The Nature of Politics

For Kant, the ultimate aim of politics is to achieve a just order of perpetual peace. This ideal requires extending the ideals of politics to the international sphere. Kant thinks that a peaceful confederation of republics represents the best possibility for this ideal. However, the political ideal of perpetual peace is not attainable, but we can approach it. Indeed, to understand history, we must assume that there is a purpose or plan in the unfolding of events. Kant does not mean that there is such a plan, but only that without this idea, history cannot be understood. Since persons have a free-will, we can assume that the plan of nature is our education towards a state of freedom and rationality. History is a process towards greater freedom, but this does not mean that all change is in fact progress.

Despite its necessary connection to morality, the doctrine of law or politics is different from the doctrine of virtue. Morality, as a form of virtue, makes demands on our will and inner motivation. The law makes demands on our external actions, not on our motivation. According to Kant, as a consequence of this difference, political duties are always perfect duties towards others. They are not duties to oneself and politics does not include imperfect duties to others, such as acts of benevolence. The purpose of politics should not be to make people happy and, benevolent despotism cannot be justified on such grounds. Therefore, we can say that law is concerned with the outer and enforceable aspect of perfect moral duties to others.

Conclusion

As a way to understand both moral and political theory, Kant's ethics explicitly and systematically articulates the Enlightenment vision of individuals as autonomous beings, which has its roots in Locke. As such it has, and continues to have, considerable influence. As a moral theory, it constitutes a major alternative to 19th century Utilitarianism, which defines the morality of an action in terms of its benefits. As a political theory, it constitutes a major alternative to 19th century socialism and Marxism. In terms of Kant's overall project, his moral theory defines a way to transform the theoretically negative notion of noumena into a positive practical concept.

22

Kant: Toward Romanticism

The idea of noumenal freedom is theoretically empty, but yet it has moral content. This separation of the theoretical and moral is necessary to make both possible: the natural world is causally ordered; morality requires freedom.

However, there is a problem given this sharp separation of theory and practice. The separation seems to entail that moral prescriptions apply only to the noumenal will. But, if this is so, how can they be applicable to our actions in the natural world? Without an answer to this question, the moral law seems irrelevant to our lives in the world as described by scientific theory.

The main aim of the *Critique of Judgment* is to resolve this difficulty. In other words, the problem of the third *Critique* is how can the noumenal idea of freedom have content for phenomenal beings? How can morality be applicable to the natural world?

Kant's solution is that we can only hope that phenomenalized morality is possible, but this hope is justified by our feeling that the natural world is beautiful. It is so justified because the feeling of beauty requires that we regard nature as though it has a purpose. In brief, the feeling of beauty leads us to regard the natural word as an expression of something supersensible or noumenal. This does not mean that the world really has a purpose, but rather only that we are compelled to view it in that way. We are compelled to so view it because this is a requirement of our scientific judgements.

In this way, the *Critique of Judgment* attempts to show how the theoretical and practical are combined in human feeling. The third Critique has two parts. The first explains how beauty is possible because of the form of purpose and, as such, is concerned with formal teleological judgment. The second part is concerned with purpose in nature, or material teleological judgments. The theme that unifies the two parts is that we need to regard nature as more than a mechanical system, namely as an expression of something supersensible, and this need arises because of the practice of science. The faculty of judgment has to make certain assumptions about nature in order for scientific investigation to be possible. Quite independently, that same assumption is required for phenomenalized morality to be possible.

The Nature of Judgment

We understand nature by positing general principles and classifications that explain natural phenomena, or, in Kant's terminology, reflective judgment aims to discover universals, which apply to particulars. According to Kant, in ascending from the particular to the universal, judgment needs to assume a priori that nature is understandable for beings like us, for example, that causal laws can be explained by a small number of more general causal principles. This a priori assumption of judgment does not determine how the world actually is, but only how we should view it. We should view the world as comprehensible for finite minds like ours.

Kant's characterization of the principle of judgment has two elements. The first represents nature as being understandable for us, for example, because of the unity of empirical causal laws The second is shaped by the quasi-teleological: the idea that we must regard nature as if it were designed.

a) The first element: In attempting to understand the world, we should adopt the general working assumption that nature is understandable. This constitutes a standard for judgment. For example, we might use the idea of the simplicity of nature to guide our investigations. Without such a standard, we can have no hope of gaining systematic empirical knowledge. The principle thus sets a goal that is functionally necessary for investigation. As it is only a heuristic guide, we do not pretend that nature does conform to that standard.

From this general assumption, we can derive more exact and specific predictions or claims about nature, which can be confirmed or falsified, even though the general principle itself cannot. When the specific predictions are falsified through observation, we should not therefore abandon the general principle, but rather continue our inquiry hoping to reveal a unity or simplicity in nature at a deeper level. Because the general principle makes a claim about what we can do, such as unifying the multifarious empirical laws of physics, it can't be definitely falsified. When it appears to be contravened, there could always be more evidence at a deeper level that shows that it is not.

b) The second element of judgment's a priori principle is teleological: the idea of the formal finality of nature. Kant says that we must regard nature as if it were designed. This is more than a functional working assumption; it is a perceptual viewpoint projected onto the world. It tells us that we must regard nature as though it were designed and were a huge work of art expressing the noumenal. In holding a quasi-teleological view of nature, one does not attribute any specific properties to the world. Formal finality is not a property of nature.

Judgment's assumption is a priori in that it is a necessary condition of gaining systematic empirical knowledge. Furthermore, to assume that nature is incomprehensible would be to surrender the idea of rational inquiry.

Beauty

According to Kant, aesthetic delight is unique amongst pleasures because it is disinterested. A beautiful object arouses our delight without appeal to our desires or will. Hence, the subject cannot find the ground of this pleasure in any idiosyncratic desires. Furthermore, aesthetic pleasure must be grounded in something common to every person and, consequently, the subject must believe that he or she has a reason for attributing a similar aesthetic pleasure to everyone. From this, Kant concludes that we demand universal and necessary agreement from others concerning what is beautiful. If I judge something to be beautiful, I implicitly claim that others ought to find it so too (and that, if they do not then, they are in some sense mistaken). For this reason, Kant says that it is as if aesthetic judgments were objective.

What makes a natural object beautiful? Kant's answer has three levels. The first is negative: Kant denies that we can answer this question by appealing to any determinate concept or set of rules that lay down when an object is beautiful. Despite his claim that aesthetic judgments demand universal agreement, Kant denies that they are strictly objective. To judge that an object is beautiful, I must rely on my own feelings, rather than on any rules or determinate concepts.

Second, Kant's positive answer is based on judgment's a priori assumption that nature is understandable. An object is beautiful when our perception of it leads us to feel justified in regarding nature as comprehensible. This consists in viewing nature as if it had been created by an intelligence other than ours for that very purpose, so that our understanding feels at home. A beautiful object makes us feel justified in regarding nature as though it were created for a purpose, although no specific purpose of ours is involved in aesthetic judgments. In other words, the beautiful encapsulates purposefulness without any actual purpose.

Third, Kant adds a psychological slant to his teleological answer. When we perceive something beautiful, our faculties synthesize the raw data of perception in an especially smooth and harmonious fashion. Aesthetic pleasure is based on the harmonious functioning of the faculties. We perceive a beautiful rose as something perfect, or just right, because we feel as if its form or shape embodies some purpose, and this results in the disinterested pleasure of beauty.

From Beauty Back to Morality

Kant maintains that the transition between the phenomenal and noumenal is made possible by the idea of finality. How does it do that? If we view the world through the eyes of finality, we shall regard it as amenable to the phenomenalization of morality and also as beautiful. As explained earlier, Kant thinks we ought to regard nature in this way because of the requirements of scientific practice. Because the feeling of beauty gives us the hope that morality can be phenomenalized, we have a moral interest in the beauty of the world. This does not mean that beauty is reducible to morality.

As well as saying that we have a moral interest in the beautiful, Kant claims that beauty symbolizes the morally good. Beauty requires the idea of the form of purposefulness. This idea of form requires the idea of a noumenal will. The beautiful is a symbol of the good because the concept of beauty requires the hypothetical supposition of a noumenal will that designs nature in order to make it understandable for creatures cognitively constituted like us. Because a will should be considered morally good, natural beauty symbolizes the good by analogy with it.

The Sublime

Kant also analyses another kind of aesthetic pleasure, the sublime, which is afforded by contemplating the noumenal Ideas of Reason. Whereas only the Ideas of Reason may be strictly called sublime, things in nature that lead to the contemplation of these Ideas may be regarded as sublime in a derivative sense. When nature does violence to our faculties, the mind is enticed away from the sensible world towards the supersensible Ideas of Reason within, and this causes us pleasure. When nature is wild, irregular, powerful and mighty, and seems to run counter to our faculties, it is initially repellent to the mind. However, at the same time, we have a heightened awareness of the inadequacy of the sensible world in representing the Ideas, which we are led to contemplate with disinterested pleasure.

There are important differences between the beautiful and the sublime: with the beautiful, we find finality in nature; with the sublime, we find it in the supersensible Ideas of Reason. Yet these two aesthetic feelings have much in common. Both are pleasing on their own account, and in neither case does the delight depend upon our interests or upon any definite concept. Furthermore, both kinds of judgment are subjective and yet universally valid although, in the case of sublimity, Kant says that universal and necessary agreement can only be demanded through the moral law.

Teleology

In the second part of the *Critique of Judgment*, Kant examines the idea that there are purposes manifested in nature. He distinguishes external and internal purposes, but he rejects the idea that there are external purposes in nature. For example, we assert that the grass exists for the reindeer to eat and, the reindeer for the hunters, but such judgments cannot be justified.

In contrast, organisms do show internal purpose. For example, consider the growth of a tree. The tree organizes matter in a process of self-production, and this process depends on a mutual dependency of whole and part. The tree as a whole needs the leaves which it itself produces. Something has its own internal purpose when it is cause and effect of itself in two ways. First, in a purposive whole, 'each part exists by means of all the other parts and is regarded as existing for the sake of the whole' (286). Of course, this is not sufficient to distinguish an organic whole from an artifact such as a watch. This is why Kant adds the second condition: the being must be self-organizing, in the sense that the parts must be regarded as reciprocally producing each other. In summary, Kant claims that organisms are beings that show internal purpose. 'An organized product of nature is one in which everything is reciprocally end and means.'

This idea of the ends of nature is a necessary guiding principle in our scientific study. Scientists who 'dissect plants and animals' seek to investigate their structure and 'see into the reasons why the parts have such and such a position' (376). This principle is a regulative idea of judgment that we need for interpreting nature, which requires us to regard nature as governed by more than by blind causal mechanisms. This does not mean that natural events have supersensible causes, in addition to their natural causes, for that would contradict the letter and spirit of the first *Critique*. He means that mechanical causes in nature have to be also viewed teleologically (377).

Kant thinks that the idea of finality can be extended so as to interpret nature itself as a system of ends. Using the idea as a regulative principle, we can unify the whole of nature as a single system analogous to a vast organism. However, this does not justify us asserting that nature really does have a purpose. The idea of purpose is only a regulative principle of reflective judgment. Consequently, this idea gives us no reason to affirm the existence of God.

Are mechanical laws on their own sufficient to explain natural phenomena? Kant generates an apparent antinomy in reply to this question. On the one hand, the first maxim of judgment affirms that they are sufficient. On the other hand, organic beings have to be characterized using the idea of internal purpose. This apparently means that mere mechanical causality is not sufficient to make judgments about them. Consequently, the second maxim of judgment claims that some things in nature are possible but not solely because of mechanical causation. Kant calls this apparent contradiction the antinomy of teleological judgment. He resolves it by denying that there really is a contradiction. The two maxims of judgment are merely principles of investigation, and are not constitutive of the phenomenal world.

Romanticism

As modern philosophy grew towards the Enlightenment, Romanticism developed as an alternative to scientific Rationalism and Empiricism. Kant's third *Critique* was an important source of inspiration for later 19th century romantics, such as Goethe, Shelly, Wordsworth, and Byron.

Romanticism in the modern period consists in a combination of four elements. First, there is the claim that human feeling is more important that reason. Among the moderns, Pascal first expressed this idea explicitly, but. Hume articulates the point more systematically by arguing that our feelings have a more important role in the judgements we make than does reason. The second element is Rousseau's contrast between the corrupting influence of civilization and the purity of the state of nature, thereby denying the Protestant idea of natural sin and the Enlightenment view of progress. The third element is a Romantic view of nature as something almost divine. As a consequence, we should not study nature scientifically in order to manipulate it for human benefit; instead, we should seek spiritual union with it. This aspect of Romanticism was inspired by. Spinoza's identification of God with Nature and by Kant's third *Critique,* which regards nature as a whole as analogous to an organism.

Finally, Romanticism implied a new approach to self-understanding, which was exemplified by Rousseau's autobiographical *Confessions*, in which he describes frankly his fears, hopes, and emotions. The *Confessions* had a tremendous impact on later thinkers because it offered a way of understanding the individual that was directly opposed to the Empiricist and Rationalist ideals of science.

Mainly because of the influence of Rousseau, Romanticism became an important philosophical and popular movement in the 19th century, which opposed the Rationalism of Voltaire and the Enlightenment. We can discern the influence of Romanticism on 19th century thinkers, such as Kierkegaard (1813-55) and Nietzsche (1844-1900), who inspired 20th century existentialism and postmodern critiques of the Enlightenment.

Overall Conclusion

We now need to briefly review Kant's philosophy as a whole. We can divide his reconciliation of science and ethics into three steps.

1) Science requires an understanding of experience that is considerably richer than that postulated by Empiricism. It requires the a priori forms, which cannot be derived from experience. Furthermore, this new understanding destroys the notion that we are imprisoned in the subjectivity of our own ideas. We directly perceive the real world of objects in space and time.

However, Kant's richer understanding of experience does nothing to vindicate traditional rational metaphysics. The absolute conception of an unconditioned reality implicit in such metaphysics contravenes the principle that our theoretical concepts have sense only in application to the objects of possible experience, which are necessarily conditional on or relative to the a priori forms of experience. At the same time, to be able even to point out this relativity implies the empty idea of the noumenal. Because science requires transcendental idealism to explain the order in the world as expressed by synthetic a priori truths, it necessitates the negative concept of the noumenal.

2) However, this otherwise empty and negative idea of the noumenal must have a positive moral content in relation to ethical practice because noumenal freedom is a precondition of morality. In this way, Kant argues for a dualism of meaning: there are two kinds of sense: theoretical and practical. Theoretical meaning is derived from structured experience; it makes science possible and metaphysics impossible. Practical content derives from the practice of morality, which underwrites both the conception of ourselves as free autonomous beings and an ethical understanding of religion. Kant is at pains to emphasize that this dualism is not ontological; there are not two kinds of existence. Moreover, he is at pains to maintain the separation of theoretical and practical meaning. In other words, religious and metaphysical claims can have no theoretical sense.

3) However, these two kinds of sense must be united in some way, otherwise moral practice would have no meaning for our lives. Kant's third point is that the practice of science requires us to view nature as a teleological system of ends. We have no option but to regard the causal mechanisms of nature as if they worked for a purpose, otherwise, there would be no possibility of understanding organisms. Furthermore, the feeling of beauty gives us the hope that the natural universe is our home and suitable for the realization of a moral life. In other words, this feeling gives us the sense that we are not mistaken in viewing nature as the expression of something absolute. This does not mean that there are two worlds. Rather, it means that we are justified in thinking that this spatio-temporal world, which we necessarily view mechanically, should be viewed also non-mechanically, as a system of ends. We are compelled to view this world and our actions as more than mechanical for reasons quite apart from morality, because of the practice of science.

How can the scientific worldview be reconciled with the claims of morality and religion? Kant's answer is very different from Descartes' dualism. Kant does not assert that there are two worlds, the noumenal and the phenomenal. There is only one world, which is this causally determined world of things in space and time. Yet, we are compelled to regard this world and, more importantly, ourselves and our actions in another way: in accordance with the idea of freedom.

23

Grand Conclusion: A Failed Project?

It is time to review critically the story of modern philosophy as told in this book, and to try to draw some philosophical conclusions about its significance and limitations. Such a review is bound to consist in generalities. The weakness, and strength, of generalizations is that they simplify.

We divided modern philosophy into three phases in order to emphasize certain trends. The first phase, until 1700, is generally characterized by an explicit effort by the modern thinkers to escape from medieval Scholasticism and develop the concepts necessary for science. At the same time, many of the early modern thinkers were concerned about the religious, ethical and political implications of their views.

In the second phase, until 1750, Scholasticism was no longer a threat and science was more able to stand on its own feet. Therefore, we see a more critical attitude to the metaphysics of science, and the development of alternative metaphysical systems. We also noted a combination of very tightly reasoned arguments and counter-intuitive conclusions in some of the major thinkers of the period. This is the result of increased philosophical self-confidence and of a greater contrast between the Rationalism and Empiricism. These points suggest the urgent need for a reconciling synthesis based on deeper principles, which was provided by Kant.

In the third phase, the French Enlightenment philosophers engaged in open criticism of Christian doctrines and culture, publicly advocating freedom of thought. The idea of the rational and autonomous individual was expressed as new political ideals. Finally, at the end of the period, Kant tried to draw together and harmonize the many strands of modern philosophy into one grand vision.

Some Characteristics of Modern Philosophy

1) According to the medieval conception, a personal, purposive and intelligent God continuously directs the universe. In contrast, many of the moderns tended to conceive of the universe impersonally and as governed by causal laws without purpose.

2) During the medieval period, the universe was conceived as having a hierarchy, which required a distinction between the earthly and the celestial. During the modern period, this hierarchy and distinction was replaced by a single conception of matter. Qualitative differences can be explained in quantitative terms.

3) These first two points suggest the need to rethink the nature of the mind. As matter becomes conceived as something inert, the conscious nature of the mind becomes more apparent. Consequently, a general feature of the modern period is the conception of the mind as essentially having conscious ideas that represent reality. However, the views of Leibniz and Kant differ from this picture and, furthermore, they alter this conception by distinguishing between consciousness and self-consciousness.

4) Medieval thinkers tended to appeal to authorities that were given divinely revealed knowledge to support their views. In contrast, modern philosophers posited sense experience and reason as the sources of knowledge. Increasingly, claims not based on one of these sources were regarded skeptically and, thus, knowledge has limits.

5) The development of science brought to Europe a greater sense of self-confidence. It was also part and parcel of a huge political change. The continent went from a Catholic empire to a conglomeration of squabbling nation states. These changes indicated the need to rethink political theory. This reconceptualization consisted in replacing an authoritarian and divinely sanctioned political framework with a rational and mutually beneficial social contract between autonomous beings with individual rights. There is a corresponding change in the conception of morality: from obedience to God to living in accord with enlightened rationality.

One of the main consequences of the above points is that modern philosophers embrace life in this world, rather than regarding it as a temporary and uncomfortable waiting room for the next life, as the medieval thinkers tended to. This change is reflected in different ways in the views of Bacon and Spinoza who respectively stress control of nature and of oneself. Both of these views are present in the Enlightenment ideal of progress.

Two Inventions and Two Problems

Two of the major conceptual inventions of the modern period are 1) the notion of inert matter governed by mechanical and mathematically describable causal laws and, 2) the idea that knowledge must be based on the systematic observation of nature and rational principles. These two concepts underpin the modern scientific revolution and lead to the final break with Scholasticism.

These inventions bring with them two major problems. First, how can the first idea (i.e. that of inert matter) be reconciled with the description of a person as a conscious being with an autonomous free will? And, second, how can both conceptual inventions be reconciled with religious belief?

These questions were new. The medieval philosophers, who worked within the framework of the Catholic Church and had no conception of inert matter, did not face such questions. Neither, for the most part, did the ancient philosophers. The exception is the classical atomists, such as Democritus and Lucretius and, in their case, the two problems were not so severe because they did not operate within the setting of Christian doctrine.

The two basic questions of the modern period are philosophically important. Modern science promises both a clear understanding of the natural world and many material benefits. With Newton and the beginnings of the Industrial Revolution, apparently it had begun to fulfill these promises. On the other hand, modern science seems to threaten morality and other meaningful ways of understanding ourselves. Within the space of a 150 years, humanity went from being a child living at the center of God's garden, with the promise of eternal life, to being a young adult living amongst dead matter in a vast empty space, unclear even as to his own nature or identity.

As the modern period advanced, the attitude towards the two problems altered. The two questions diverged and, as thought grew more secular, the second problem, concerning religion, became less of a priority compared to the first, concerning humans. Furthermore, the development of the new ethical and political vision makes the first problem seem especially acute. This vision required the assumption that the individual is able to make free, rational and self-conscious choices and this assumption seemed incompatible with mechanistic science.

Three Solutions

In very general terms, the modern philosophers had three basic strategies for answering these two questions.

1) First, there is a skeptical monist solution. This may take the form of materialism, as adopted by Hobbes. Science requires only the existence of matter and, therefore, there must be a scientifically based justification of consciousness and freedom. To the extent that our religious and moral conceptions do not fit into this scientific framework, then so much the worse for them. They must be altered. Hume adopts another form of a skeptical monist solution based on his epistemology of impressions and ideas. All concepts must be based on impressions. The resulting skepticism is even more profound.

2) Second, there is the non-skeptical monist, or the idealist, answer. Matter as described by science does not really exist, or at least it is a derivative concept, and we can explain science reasonably well without it. Mental substance is the fundamental existent and, on this basis, religion, consciousness and morality are preserved. Leibniz and Berkeley clearly opt for this kind of strategy.

3) Third, there is dualism. Descartes argued for an ontological mind/body dualism, but this tempting theory surprisingly turns out to be one of the least accepted of the modern solutions, and for good reasons. The alternative is to argue for a sophisticated non-ontological meaning dualism in the way that Kant does. According to this idea, there are not two kinds of reality, but rather two kinds of meaning: the theoretical meaning found in scientific judgments and the practical meaning inherent in our practice of morality.

This neat scheme does not fit all the modern philosophers. Locke seems to hover between the first and third options. Despite the fact that he does not either accept or reject Descartes' mind/body dualism, Locke's philosophy seems to require an idea/matter dualism. On the other hand, he argues skeptically that certain ideas, such as the positive notion of the infinite, cannot be justified empirically and, in this sense, his position is similar to Hume's. Spinoza could be classified as adopting both the second and third options. His dual aspect theory might be considered a form of dualism. However, he also he denies the existence of material substance and, in this way and others, he seems more like an idealist. The fact that some philosophers do not fit the classification is not really a problem; we can simply note that for example, Spinoza in some ways fits one category and, in other ways, fits another.

The point of the classification is that each of these positions has its own characteristic problems, which we shall briefly review.

1) Skeptical monism: The fundamental problems this view faces are 'Can we justify our notions of the conscious and rational self within a materialist or a radical empiricist framework?' and 'If not, can we really eliminate them?' If the answer to both questions is no, then skeptical monism is false. For example, is Hume's notion of the self as a bundle of perceptions an adequate conception of a person? If it is not, and if that is the only notion of the self that can be derived from Hume's empiricism, then we must challenge his starting premises. Similar questions apply to materialism.

2) Idealistic monism faces the fundamental question 'Can the nature of scientific knowledge really be adequately explained without regarding the idea of inert matter as basic or fundamental?' For example, can Berkeley adequately explain how different minds perceive in a similar way in the same situation without the thesis that people perceive common public material objects rather than their own private ideas? Is Leibniz's explanation of the harmony of the perceptions and appetites of the monads adequate, given that he cannot appeal to the notion of matter?

3) Dualism suffers from the problem that the two elements that the dualist wants to separate have to be brought together. For example, Descartes distinguishes mind and body and thereby invents the modern notions of inert matter and the conscious mind. Having separated them, he needs to recombine them in order to understand human existence (see Chapter 5). Likewise, Kant tries to distinguish theoretical and practical meaning in order to save the practice of morality from the mechanical nature of science without embracing traditional theoretical metaphysics. However, he has to reunite them to make morality relevant to this world and, hence, Kant argues for the teleological theses of the third *Critique*. The fundamental question facing dualism is 'Can the two elements once separated be recombined without contradiction? For example, does Descartes' notion of a substantial union of mind-body be reconciled with his dualism? For instance, does Kant's analysis of beauty explain how noumenal moral notions can be applied to some phenomenal events, namely our actions?

Of course, pointing out the problems with a view does not constitute an argument against a thesis. It merely indicates a possible line of argumentation. Furthermore, the questions that I have raised are very far from exhaustive.

A Failed Project?

In fact, in the contemporary philosophical literature, there are many detailed critiques of the presuppositions, arguments and conclusions of each of the modern philosophers. However, in this work, we have not tried to evaluate critically their claims, although we have indicated some of the ways in which modern philosophers might criticize each other. Therefore, it is appropriate to mention very briefly three general kinds of critiques, which are distinct from the questions that are raised above, and from the criticisms given by the modern philosophers themselves.

1) Empiricism

The Empiricist claim that an individual can perceive only his or her own ideas seems to imprison the subject within the private world of his or her experiences. In contrast, most contemporary philosophers stress that we live in and have direct access to a public and shared world of objects and other people. In other words, we can directly perceive objects and others. Furthermore, by arguing that all ideas are derived from experience, the Empiricists make all concepts and meaning essentially private and, thereby, deny the social and public nature of language, which is necessary for communication. Third, in so doing, the Empiricists tend to regard ideas as private mental items. They approach perception as the having of pictures in the mind that represent reality. This reifies mental contents or treats them as items or things. In contrast, many contemporary philosophers see this as a muddle. It confuses the content of a perceiving with the object perceived. Furthermore, they argue that the very concept of a picture that represents reality is flawed. A belief about reality is not a neutral reproduction of what exists, because all beliefs must be framed in terms of social and historically developed concepts.

2) Rationalism

Rationalism supposes that nature has a rational order, which human reason is able to grasp. Thus, it presents a non-historical and universal notion of reason that is supposed to apply equally to both physical causes and human behavior. In this way, it fails to distinguish adequately between the natural causes of events and the reasons for human behavior, and fails to take into account the historical and social nature of both. In the case of scientific explanations of physical events, it ignores that what counts as an adequate physical explanation may alter as scientific concepts change. In the case of reasons for human action, it overlooks the social, and historical factors that make actions intelligible, and under-emphasizes the non-rational. It tends to disregard the important point that the interpretation of an action must take into account the perspective of the agent who performed the action. We can see this positive point reflected in Rousseau's *Confessions* and articulated in Herder's philosophy of history (see Chapter 19), and appreciation of the point led to the development of the social sciences in the 19th century.

3) Enlightenment
The Enlightenment conception of a person as an autonomous individual has been put into question in the 20th century and, as a consequence, so have political and moral theories based on such a conception. In particular, this Enlightenment conception of the person has been criticized for ignoring the importance of social relations and historical factors. Society is more than a political contract between autonomous individuals in part because we are linguistic beings that employ concepts, which are necessarily social and historical. In brief, the Enlightenment conception stresses our independence at the cost of ignoring our interdependence.

For these reasons among many others, there is a tendency among some contemporary philosophers to regard modern philosophy as a failed project. In light of the above briefly outlined criticisms one can see why. Philosophy has changed very fundamentally since the modern period. Nevertheless, there are three reasons for doubting that modern philosophy can be viewed fairly as a failure.

1) At least one of its central problems is still with us. As we saw earlier, one basic problem of modern philosophy is how to reconcile physical science with our understanding of ourselves. This problem still infests much contemporary 20th century thought. The problem is still with us today, though in a very different form. The problem is now less often tied to religion. Furthermore, the modern philosophers sought to answer this problem in the areas of metaphysics and epistemology. In contemporary philosophy, the problem tends to be framed in terms of meaning. It underlies many discussions in the philosophy of language and mind as well as in debates about the nature of understanding in the social and natural sciences.

In a way, this 20th century debate seems more acute. On the one hand, during the 20th century, there is much more skepticism about science's apparent ability to describe the world objectively. Furthermore, there is much more concern about the cultural, political, ecological and technological effects of science. On the other hand, science has developed tremendously since Newton. In particular, Darwin has presented a way to understand biological processes mechanically. Nevertheless, in summary, if one of the central problems of modern philosophy is still with us today, albeit in a very different form, we cannot portray the work of the moderns as a failure.

2) There is no doubt that, for better or worse, the modern philosophers brought about many revolutionary changes in human thinking. One of their main aims was to escape Scholasticism and, in this respect, they succeeded. Another aim was to develop a unified vision of the natural sciences, and in this respect too they succeeded. In other words, given the historically situated aims they had, their project did not fail.

3) At the beginning of the 21st century, we confront the problems of global poverty, ecological degradation and worldwide social problems. Perhaps, we feel the need for a more human based and less technological and commercial culture and conception of progress. In these conditions, it is natural that we should question the limits of scientific understanding and that we should try to escape some of the fundamental assumptions of modern philosophy. In other words, we face new problems and need new ideas to cope with them. Therefore, we are bound to rethink modern philosophy and try to shun some of its basic premises. We are still in the process of working out which of the assumptions of the modern period need to be discarded. However, in the attempt to sort out the understandings appropriate for our new historical condition, we should not forget that the modern philosophers were trying to do precisely the same with respect to the earlier medieval period.

Bibliography

General Works

Atherton, Margaret, *Women Philosophers of the Early Modern Period*, Hackett Publishing, 1994

Bennett, Jonathan, *Learning from Six Philosophers*, Clarendon Press, 2001

Cottingham, J., *The Rationalists*, Oxford University Press, 1988

Garber, Daniel and Ayers, M. eds., *The Cambridge History of 17th Century philosophy*, Cambridge University Press, 1998

Schacht, Richard, *Classical Modern Philosophers: Descartes to Kant*, Routledge, 1993

Thomson, Garrett, *Bacon to Kant: an Introduction to Modern Philosophy*, Waveland Press, 2001

Woolhouse, R. S, *The Empiricists*, Oxford University Press, 1988

The Rise of Science

Matthews, Michael, ed. *The Scientific Background to Modern Philosophy,* Hackett Publishing, 1989

Casper, Max, *Kepler*, Dover Publications, 1993

Dyksterhuis, E.J., *The Mechanization of the World Picture*, Princeton, 1986

Drake, Stillman, *Galileo at Work: His Scientific Biography*, University of Chicago Press, 1978

Bacon

Faulkner, R.K., *Francis Bacon and the Project of Progress*, Rowman and Littlefield, 1993

Perez-Ramos, *Francis Bacon's Idea of Science*, Oxofrd University Press, 1988

Quinton, Anthony, *Francis Bacon*, Oxford, 1980

Descartes

Cottingham, John, *Descartes*, Basil Blackwell, 1986

Cottingham, John, ed., *The Cambridge Companion to Descartes*, Cambridge, 1992

Gaukroger, Stephen, *Descartes: An Intellectual Biography*, Clarendon Press, 1997

Kenny, Anthony, *Descartes*, Random House, New York, 1968

Sorrell, Tom, *Descartes,* Oxford University Press, 1987

Thomson, Garrett, *On Descartes,* Wadsworth, 2000

Williams, Bernard, *Descartes: The Project of Pure Enquiry*, Penguin, 1978

Early Modern French Philosophy

Radner, D., *Malebranche*, Van Gorcum, 1978

Screech, M.A., *Montaigne and Melancholy*, Duckworth, 1983

Miel, Jan, *Pascal and Theology*, John Hopkins, 1969

Hobbes

Martinich, A.P., *Thomas Hobbes*, St. Martins Press, 1997

Peters, R.S., *Hobbes,* Penguin Books, 1967

Sorrel, Tom, *Hobbes,* Routledge and Kegan Paul, 1986

Spinoza

Allison, Henry, *Benedict de Spinoza: An Introduction*, Yale, 1987

Bennett, Jonathan, *A Study of Spinoza's Ethics,* Hackett, 1985

Curley, E.M., *Spinoza's Metaphysics,* Cambridge, 1969

Hampshire, Stuart, *Spinoza,* Baltimore, 1962

Parkinson, H.R., *Spinoza's Theory of Knowledge*, Oxford, 1954

Scruton, R., *Spinoza,* Oxford, 1986

Newton

Cohen, Bernard, *The Newtonian Revolution*, Cambridge, 1980

Thayer, H.S., *Newton's Philosophy of Nature* (selections), Hafner Publishing, 1953

Locke

Ayers, M., *Locke* (2 Vols), Routledge, 1991

Chappell, V., *The Cambridge Companion to Locke*, Cambridge, 1994

Dunn, J., *Locke*, Oxford, 1984

Jolley, N., *Locke: His Philosophical Thought*, Oxford, 1999

Mackie, John, *Problems from Locke*, Oxford, 1976

Thomson, Garrett, *On Locke*, Wadsworth, 2001

Woolhouse, R.S., *Locke*, Brighton, 1983
Yolton, J., *Locke; an Introduction*, Oxford, 1985

Leibniz
Adams, Robert Merrihew, *Leibniz: Determinist, Theist, Idealist*, Oxford, 1994
Brown, Stuart, *Leibniz*, University of Minnesota, 1984
Mates, Benson, *The Philosophy of Leibniz*, Oxford, 1986
Jolley, N. (ed.), *The Cambridge Companion to Leibniz*, 1995
Parkinson, G.H.R., *Logic and Reality in Leibniz' Metaphysics*, Garland, 1985
Rescher, Nicholas, *Leibniz: an Introduction to his philosophy*, Blackwell, 1979
Ross, George MacDonald, *Leibniz*, Oxford, 1984
Thomson, Garrett, *On Leibniz*, Wadsworth, 2000

Berkeley
Dancy, Jonathan, *Berkeley: An Introduction*, Basil Blackwell, 1987
Pitcher, George, *Berkeley*, Routledge, 1977
Tipton, I.C., *Berkeley: The Philosophy of Immaterialism*, London Methuen, 1974
Urmson, J.O., *Berkeley*, Oxford University Press, 1982
Warnock, G.J., *Berkeley*, Pelican, Harmondsworth, 1953
Winkler, K.P., *Berkeley: An Interpretation*, Oxford, 1989

Hume
Baier, Annette, *A Progress of Sentiments: Reflections on Hume's Treatise,* Harvard University Press, 1991
Pears, David, *Hume's System*, Oxford, 1990
Quinton, A., *Hume,* Routledge, 1999
Strawson, G., *The Secret Connexion: Realism and David Hume*, Oxford, 1989
Stroud, Barry, *Hume*, Routledge, 1977

Voltaire
Peter Gilmour, ed., *Philosophers of the Enlightenment*, Barnes & Noble Books, 1990
Ayer, A.J., *Voltaire*, Random House, 1986

Rousseau
Grimsley, Ronald, *The Philosophy of Rousseau*, Oxford University Press, 1973

Melzer, Arthur M, *The Natural Goodness of Man: on the system of Rousseau's thought*, University of Chicago Press, 1990
Wokler, Robert, *Rousseau*, Oxford University Press, 1995

Kant

Allison, Henry, *Kant's Transcendental Idealism*, Yale, 1983
Bennett J., *Kant's Dialectic*, Cambridge, 1974
Crawford, D., *Kant's Aesthetic Theory*, University of Wisconsin Press, 1974
Guyer, P., *The Cambridge Companion to Kant*, Cambridge, 1992
Guyer, P., *Kant and the Claims of Knowledge*, Cambridge, 1987
Scruton, Roger, *Kant*, Oxford, 1982
Strawson, Sir Peter, *The Bounds of Sense*, Metheun 1966
Thomson, Garrett, *On Kant*, Wadsworth, 2000
Walker, Ralph, *Kant*, Routledge, 1979
Wood, Allen, *Kant's Moral Religion*, Cornell, 1970